1000 Best
New Teacher
Survival
Secrets

Kathleen Brenny
and
Kandace Martin

 Sou

D1041412

Published by Sourcebooks, Inc.
P.O. Box 4410, Naperville, Illinois 60567-4410
(630) 961-3900
FAX: (630) 961-2168
www.sourcebooks.com

Library of Congress Cataloging-in-Publication Data
Brenny, Kathleen.
  1000 best new teacher survival secrets / Kathleen Brenny and
Kandace Martin.
     p. cm.
  Includes index.
  ISBN 1-4022-0550-3 (alk. paper)
  1. Effective teaching. 2. First year teachers. I. Title: One thou-
sand best new teacher survival secrets. II. Martin, Kandace. III.
Title.

LB1025.3.B75 2005
371.1—dc22   2005019862

Printed and bound in Canada
WC 10 9 8 7 6 5 4

Dedication

Dedicated to our supportive husbands—
Bill and Curt

Table of Contents

Acknowledgments

The numerous educators, students, and families that have influenced our work.

Introduction

Welcome to one of the most influential professions. It is an honor to offer tips to enhance your skills and empower you to be an exemplary teacher. We have embraced the opportunity to reflect on almost seventy collaborative years of educational experience.

As we continue to work in the field of education, we have learned through extensive reading, taking classes, collaborative interactions with colleagues, parents, and the community. The day-to-day teaching of our students and learning from them has allowed us to glean many insights. We have become sagacious by doing, by our triumphs, and our failures in schools. When we thought we had seen and heard it all, we hadn't. When we wanted to call it quits, a student reached out to us and made our day.

Our work was never finished because teaching and learning are unfinished entities. Quite frankly, education is our life and we are proud to say that we are educators.

Throughout the years, we have served in the educational arena in different capacities and have viewed education from different perspectives, but none have been more gratifying than being a classroom teacher. No other position is more critical to student learning than an effective classroom teacher. Research tells us that a teacher has a profound, positive influence on student achievement. The tips furnished in this book will help current and future teachers gain a deeper understanding of the many decisions faced by teachers, the complexities of the position, and the best practices that need to be exercised frequently. Our hope is that you will refer to our book to help you find better ways to solve problems that you'll face, to recognize a better way to do things, to enhance student learning, and to find the joy we have discovered in the very important work that needs to be done. The following tips are intended to help you maximize learning opportunities and challenge you to always think of a better way to impact learning. Pick up the book when you are searching for answers, or when you are pondering a situation. The book is filled with what we consider to be many of the pearls that will assist you in being a significant teacher and effect student learning.

We are humbled by the many talented colleagues we have worked with, the families that have entrusted their children to us, and the communities that have supported our efforts. We salute them as we salute you for your commitment to education's future.

As we have collaborated on this book, it has involved a multitude of conversations and reflections. Through the writing process we have realized a stronger and deeper love for education. We are grateful to you, the reader, for the opportunity to share our knowledge about teaching and learning with you.

1.
Getting
Started

1. Before you sign your contract, look it over carefully. Ask questions if you don't understand the language. Does the contract reflect the correct salary, extra duties, and number of days that you will be employed? Save a copy for yourself and file it in a safe place at home.

2. Call the human resource director or adminis-trator and ask for an explanation of your health plan and other benefits. Health plans vary from district to district. If you have a choice of plans, you need to be able to make an informed decision. Make a list of questions before you call the administrator so you can be sure to ask questions based on your current situation.

3. Establish as many contacts as you can before school begins. If you have questions, ask the secretaries, administrators, and other school per-sonnel. They are willing and happy to answer all sorts of questions.

4. Ask the secretaries the following questions: Where do I get the keys to my room? What is the procedure for gaining entrance to the building? May I work in the building on weekends? Where will I find a class schedule?

5. Become familiar with the layout of the build-ing, where to park, and which door to enter. Prior to the start of school, also become familiar with emergency exits and standard procedures.

6. Familiarize yourself with the neighborhood surrounding the school. You will learn more about your students and their families by taking a tour of the area and understanding the territory surrounding the school. This tour will give you a greater understanding of their lives at home and in their neighborhood before you begin to know them in the school setting.

7. Read the school mission statement, the student handbook, and the faculty handbook before school begins. When students arrive, you will be busy preparing for the week and will have little time to read about procedures and policies. You need to have a clear understanding of the policies that you and the students must adhere to. Ask the office for copies of the policies, and ask the administrator if you have any questions.

8. Inquire about the school's goals, initiatives, and how teachers implement staff development plans. If this information is not provided by the principal or administrator, ask another teacher. Knowing the strategies and the initiatives that the school is focusing on will help you effectively prepare for the school year. Ask about information provided to the teachers, materials that were given, and books that were read by the faculty. If you have this information in advance, you will be able to read and assimilate lessons that support staff development.

9. Obtain a school calendar that details not only official school days, but also days set aside for staff development seminars, parent-teacher conferences, and vacations. Transfer these dates to your planning calendar. Often teachers get so involved surviving from day to day that they forget about upcoming events and activities.

10. Introduce yourself to the custodian. Ask him or her where the hallway lights are located and other information about the physical layout of the building. Ask the custodian about the heating/cooling of the building and, in particular, in your classroom. Heat or lack of it in a classroom can impact student learning.

11. Make a list of questions that you have and schedule a time to meet with the principal or dean of students to go over discipline procedures, district goals, and contractual obligations.

12. Ask the principal or dean of students the procedure to take attendance. If the school uses a computerized attendance system, who will teach you to use the program and who is in charge of troubleshooting? Knowing this prior to the first day of school will give you ample time to browse the site and get to know the system.

13. Make an appointment with the principal or dean of students to specifically discuss how you plan to structure your classroom management plan. You will gain feedback from your discussion and you will have alerted the administrator about your plan. When you need to discipline a student, the administrator will have prior knowledge about your plan and will be able to support your actions without many questions.

14. Find out where teachers eat lunch, if you have lunch duty, where the faculty lounge is located, where to find the faculty bathrooms, and where to find the faculty mailboxes. Knowing the location of certain places will help you as you navigate around school.

15. Obtain any forms that are given by the office. Ask the secretaries which forms you will need. Place the forms in folders in your file cabinet or in your desk drawer. Remember where you put the forms, why you may need them in the classroom, and who will get the forms when they are filled out. By knowing this information you will not have to interrupt your school day to ask questions—you already know the answers.

16. Inquire about a mentoring program at your school. Many states and individual school districts will pair a veteran teacher with a first-year teacher. If your school has established a program, ask how the program is structured, including the requirements and expectations. A good mentor and an effective program lend support and guidance during a teacher's first years in the profession.

17. Inquire about sick leave and the procedure for calling in sick. Who do you call? What time does the sub caller or principal need to know that you won't be at school? Make a list of telephone numbers of school personnel that you may need to call, and keep one list at home and the other one in the car.

18. Ask if lesson plans have to be submitted to the administrator. If yes, when do they need to be submitted? Are they computer generated on a specific program, or can they be handwritten?

Organize Your Classroom

19. Visit the school you are assigned and find your classroom. If the school hasn't determined room assignments, visualize what your classroom will look like based on the other rooms. Draw a plan for your classroom including desks or tables, bulletin boards, chalk or white boards, file cabinets, and bookshelves. You will be spending a great deal of time in the room with your students. A good floor plan will prevent many classroom management problems.

20. When you are officially assigned a room, walk in and begin to make a list of your needs and wants. Take the list to the principal and ask about the procedure for getting bookshelves, file cabinets, and bulletin boards. To make your room conducive for learning, you do need the basics.

21. Structure a welcoming environment for your students. Designate a specific place to display student work, hang posters, and arrange student pictures. Designate areas for students to read, areas for students to use the computer, areas for projects, areas for learning stations, an area for books/magazines, and an area where you talk to students about behavior issues. Students will associate a designated area with a particular activity.

22. Organize the materials in your classroom, label them, cover tattered bulletin boards, and clean the areas that need to be cleaned, including the doorknobs. Work to make this an appealing place for learning. Students will take care of the classroom if they know you care about the room, and you will want to come to work if you like being in the room.

23. As you rearrange your room, keep in mind that the room needs to be uncluttered. Rooms that have every inch of space covered often overstimulate students to the point that they cannot focus in the chaos. Keep in mind, however, a room with only a few commercial posters that may not have anything to do with learning can be cold and uninviting for the learner.

24. If you are teaching from a cart, decorate your cart to show off your interests. Create an interesting classroom on wheels by hanging a license plate on the front, handing out posters, or putting the school's mascot in a child's seat. This will draw attention to your learning environment on wheels. Students will comment on your rover, and you will feel more a part of the school.

25. Designate areas where students can turn in their assignments or pick up assignments and materials when they were absent. Students can bombard a teacher with questions at the beginning of class. By targeting an area and adopting a procedure that students need to follow, the class will have fewer interruptions and flow more smoothly.

26. Designate an area where you post your assignments on a weekly basis. Students need to be aware of a bigger picture than a daily assignment. Students will automatically look to the posting area and know what will be happening in class. Many questions about assignments will be answered simply and efficiently with this display.

27. Designate another area for daily announcements, upcoming events, and special announcements. Students will always know where to look for the information, thus saving class time for learning instead of a myriad of questions about announcements or events.

28. Personalize your classroom by providing a setting that displays the interests, activities, and accomplishments of you and your students. Displays and memorabilia become talking points and a source of pride for the teacher and students. Check with students before asking them to bring pictures, special collections, or other artifacts. Some students are not comfortable with displaying their treasures for other students.

Preemptive Safety Measures

29. Be aware of fire codes in the building. Ask if you are allowed to hang student-made mobiles from the lights, have materials blocking an exit, or hang decorations on the ceiling or on the door. Codes are designed to protect us and we must abide by them.

30. In an older building, watch out for over-crowded outlets. Ask the custodian for guidance if you begin to need extra electrical outlets. You may not be in compliance with city codes and could be asked to unplug some of your electrical equipment.

31. Be alert of the air quality in your room. Never burn candles in your room, and beware of using room deodorizers. Some students are allergic to certain odors. If a musty smell prevails, ask the custodian to check the air. If needed, requisition an air purifier. Mold and musty odors can cause health issues. If the custodian cannot help you, talk with the school principal.

32. Contact the school nurse and ask him or her to discuss procedures for sending students to the nurse's office. Find out how students get their medication, which students in your room are on medication, and which students need to be observed for various health-related symptoms. You need to be prepared the first day of class. Obtaining information is valuable as you organize your day.

33. Keep a first aid kit in your room. Next to the first aid kit keep gloves handy. If you are allergic to latex, ask the office or nurse for an alternative type of gloves. Students do get paper cuts, bloody noses, and a few scrapes. The first aid kit will also have bandages for the minor abrasions.

34. Call on the intercom, phone, or send a student immediately to the nurse or to the principal's office if a student needs immediate assistance. Tell the other students to remain in their seats. If the student is conscious, talk to the student and reassure him or her that help is on the way. Determine among the adults who will call the student's parents/guardians.

35. Check to see that fire, tornado, and earthquake exit instructions are well marked and visible. The law states that the directions must be easy to read and visible in the room.

36. During the school year desks get grimy and dirty. If you ask students to help clean the desks, supply rubber gloves and soapy water. If you are cleaning the desks yourself, wear rubber gloves and use a disinfectant. When a learning environment feels clean to the touch, students will appreciate the work. Cleaning the desks or tables also helps to kill the germs that multiply and cause illnesses and absenteeism.

Materials You Need

37. During your visit with the principal or department head, ask about the curriculum, but specifically about the texts that are provided. As a precaution, count the number of textbooks that you have been allocated. Match the number of textbooks with the number of students you tentatively have in class. Next, count the number of desks and make sure there is a desk for every student. Each student is entitled to a desk or table. Ask the custodian or other teachers if you need more desks or tables.

38. Before purchasing a weekly or daily planner, ask the secretary if the school furnishes planners. Use daily, weekly, or monthly planners to write your lesson plans. Use your planner to also keep notes and reminders of upcoming meetings. If you are organized on paper, the class will also be organized in practice. Class time is maximized.

39. The school secretary can be your biggest ally and a great source of information. Ask the secretary what supplies you can obtain from the office. Generally the office has a closet full of supplies. If the office doesn't have the supplies you need, ask how to obtain them. Your school may have a discount program for supplies or a policy for ordering additional materials.

40. Ask how you order supplemental materials. Every school building and district has different requirements for placing such an order.

41. Ask if you can have live plants or fish in your room. Plants soften the room. Fish add a calming affect. Both offer an opportunity for students to become caregivers.

42. Ask where overheads, projectors, screens, television, and VCR/CD/DVD players are kept. Find out how they are checked out and how long you are able to keep them. Schedule ahead of time, and you won't have problems getting the equipment for a lesson.

43. In the elementary school where you are responsible for teaching several subject areas, make a list of materials that you need such as maps, science equipment, math manipulates, and games and puzzles. Next take an inventory of what you have in the closets, cabinets, and files. Check off what you have and note what you need. Approach the school principal with your requests.

44. Find out where films and videos can be ordered. You will want to look at the list and order materials to preview before school begins. Supplementing your curriculum takes planning. Using time before school starts will help you plan your units.

45. Find where the copy machine is located for the teachers. Ask if you have to have a password, how many copies can be made, if you can print on colored paper, and when peak periods for the copy machine are during the day. If you know how to operate the machine, you will lower your stress level and be more prepared for the classroom.

46. Check to see that your name and room number are clearly visible outside your room. If they are too small for a crowd of students to see the first day, make a larger sign. Personalize it with interesting books to read, quotes, or pictures. Parents will also appreciate finding a clearly identified room.

47. Make several computer-generated student labels for name tags, folders, student booklets, and coat hooks. You can use them for everything. This will save you time when you need a set of labels later in the school year.

48. Generate multiple blank checklists with your students' names on the side. You can use these for checking off who was on the computer, who went to the bathroom, who brought his or her permission slip, and who is on the bus for a field trip. The uses for the blank checklists are endless. Save yourself time and print off many.

49. Decide on a theme for your classroom for the year. The theme can carry through to posters, stickers, books, and interdisciplinary units. Examples of themes include: "Get in the learning MOOOOOOOOD" (cows), "Gr8t Expectations" (eighth grade expectations), and "Bee the Best" (bees).

Get to Know Your Students before They Arrive

50. Prepare for student learning before classes begin by reading student records, talking with the previous teacher, or attending workshops that will fuel your planning efforts. You will feel more prepared and energized for the beginning of the school year.

51. Ask the principal's office for a tentative class list after district registration, which usually is scheduled two weeks before school begins. This will give you an idea of how many students you will need to seat in the classroom. If it looks like the number of desks is insufficient, alert the principal before the first day of classes that you need more. Schools must provide an equitable education. A student without a desk is not being provided an equitable education.

52. Take time to learn the correct pronunciation and spelling of students' names in your classroom. Students immediately feel as if they belong to the class, and you begin building relationships. Learn names quickly using pictures that you have scanned onto the class list or designed to use specifically for this class. Attaching pictures and names will help you remember the students.

53. Don't write names in grade books or type them into the computer until after the first week of classes. Your roster will change. Save yourself time and wait.

54. Design lesson plans in advance. You can always change the lesson plans, but you will need a plan of action. Think about each lesson and how you might change, delete, or supplement it.

55. Be very flexible during the first week. Students are coming back from a long summer vacation; you are refocusing after an unstructured summer. The weather may not cooperate, projects at the school may not have been finished, and other things may not be to your liking. Take a deep breath. A more routine schedule will follow.

56. Arrange students in alphabetical order the first several weeks. Since you don't know the students for the first several weeks, an alphabetical placement will expedite many of the tasks you have to do.

57. Check the policy for field trips, and ask if the district has a standard permission slip or if you have to design one. If you need to design your own, be sure to include:
- The building's name, address, and phone number
- Your name and the name of the class
- Where the students are going
- Location from where they depart and return
- The date of the event
- Time they leave and will return
- If lunch is provided
- How much spending money needs to be sent, if any
- A line for the student's name
- A line for parents or guardians to sign and date
- When the permission slip needs to be returned
- Appropriate dress

58. If you are teaching in a secondary classroom, remind yourself not to judge students by the way they dress, the number of piercings they have, or the tattoos that they have inked on their bodies. Be sure to not group students by stereotype.

59. During the first week of school, teach your students the procedures for lunch. Although this is a time for camaraderie, it can also be a time for making messes and not following lunchroom rules. With younger students, review the rules daily until they can recite the rules. With older students, review as necessary until behavior is appropriate.

60. If you do not have lunch duty, consider sitting with your students or sitting at the faculty table for lunch. As you observe the students, watch who they are interacting with at the tables. This type of information helps to build a mental student profile, which may help with seating arrangements and forming groups in the classroom.

61. Take time during lunch to meander through the lunchroom and talk with students in an informal setting. They relish the attention from their teacher or former teachers. This is another time to joke with students, touch base on how they are doing, and to ask questions about their likes and dislikes. Use the opportunity to build relationships.

62. Try to get rested before you begin the first day of school. Many veteran teachers and administrators admit that their stomachs are churning in nervous anticipation. Work at having everything organized and ready to go for the first week of classes. Expect to feel exhausted every day during the first week because you are not used to a new routine or the amount of information that you need to organize.

63. Think about the first impression that you will make with students. Pay attention to your facial expressions, body language, gestures, and movements. Try to look relaxed and confident in front of the students. They have only you to focus on. They will scrutinize every piece of you. Show them the best of you the first day.

64. Plan what you will say the first day of class. Script the day and practice ahead of time. You want to show students that you know your material, that you are confident, and that you are serious about their learning. If you stumble over your words, are disorganized, or appear nervous, students will take that as a sign of weakness.

65. Provide students with an overview of what they can expect to learn in the classroom during the semester or the entire year. Summarizing the big picture helps students to better understand what is included in the curriculum and what they will be studying. Share this information in a handout and orally in class.

66. During the first day of classes, don't get glued to one spot. Move around the classroom pointing out where items are kept, how to access the computers, where to find assignments, and other pertinent information.

67. Begin each class period or each day with a variety of activities as soon as the students enter the classroom. Every minute in the classroom counts. Students and teachers both need to be held accountable for using each minute. For example, a math problem or a new vocabulary word could be written on the board, or students could write in their journals. Each activity needs to be short and should be completed within the first few minutes of class. Students need the structure that a daily routine provides to maximize their learning potential.

68. Teach students that when they enter the classroom, all personal items are to be put away and they need to check for paper, pencils, textbooks, and assignments. If a student needs to borrow a pen or pencil, have him or her leave something with you as collateral. That way you will get the writing utensil back again.

69. Focus all of your energy on your students. Relate a little information about yourself but don't tell them your life story. Plan an activity that will help you to remember student names. Tell them why you feel it is important to know something about them and why it is important to build a learning and caring environment in the classroom.

70. A scavenger hunt to familiarize students with the classroom is a great activity for the first day of school. Students can walk around and discover where things are located without you telling them. This is an example of hands-on learning, instead of students sitting and getting the information from the teacher.

71. Before the first day of class you may feel prepared, but after the first day of classes you might feel tired and overwhelmed. This is a natural feeling that many teachers experience. Veteran teachers will advise you to take one day at a time. Listen to the veteran teachers because they have been there before.

72. In the elementary grades, divide the class into "responsibility teams" that are responsible for taking lunch count, handing out papers, or picking up the room. Teach students what is expected of them with each task. Not only does this teach responsibility, but students also feel a part of the class. Make these assignments in the first week so it becomes routine.

73. In middle school and high school, teach students to routinely pick up around their area before they leave class. Students need to know that they are responsible for keeping the classroom free of debris and trash.

74. Develop procedures for getting drinks, going to the restroom, and going to the office. Let students know on the first day that you expect them to be at class on time and to have taken care of other duties. Sometimes, however, emergencies do happen and students need to know where to get a pass. The benefit of teaching procedures and routines the first week of school helps to alleviate constant interruptions during the lesson.

75. Teach students how to use the computers in your room. Students need to hear and see the school policy for accessing computers and the Internet. Find the policy in the student handbook and read it aloud to them. Ask other teachers about the consequences for accessing illicit material from the school computer. The same policy also applies to adults in the school.

76. Teach students during the first week of the school year how you want assignments to be labeled or formatted. Ask teachers in your department or grade level if there is a standardized way that all students address their papers (name, date, margins). If there is no standard way, develop your own way. This simplifies the grading process.

77. Think about how you will return student work. Individual work is a private matter between the student and the teacher. Grades need to remain confidential. Always be the one person who distributes graded papers. Place them face down on the desk. Alert students ahead of time not to ask another person about the grade that he or she received.

78. Keep folders for student work in marked crates or boxes in the classroom where students have access to their own work. Students will be able to view the progress that they make from the beginning of the school year until the end. This is also an organizational technique that keeps papers together.

79. Samples of student work can be gathered for parent-teacher conferences and to show growth from the beginning of the school year until the end of the school year. Find a crate or a box to place the folders in and start collecting these items right away.

80. In elementary school alert parents when student work, announcements, and messages will be coming home with students. Ask other teachers how materials, papers, and announcements are sent home and on what day. Include a letter to parents explaining what the students are working on, and what you have planned for the future. Parents want this information. This also is a positive way to share information with parents and build connections.

81. Survey students about their interests, books that they have read, and their learning preferences. The information that you gain will help you to design appropriate lessons that support their learning style, what they like, and what they have read.

82. Determine when and how you will see students who need extra help or have questions over the material. Consider before and after school sessions, recess time, or at the end of the lunch period. Sometimes phone and email correspondence is helpful as well. Set up your procedures for additional help at the beginning of the year so students can plan accordingly.

83. Try to remove podiums from your classroom. If you must keep the podium, move in front of it. Teachers tend to hide behind it, lean on it, or read their notes from the podium. It serves as a barrier between you and the students. Free yourself from it.

84. As you begin working at school, take the first step and introduce yourself to other teachers. Because time is at a premium for every teacher before classes begin, stay a short time, ask a quick question, get the answer, and leave to resume your own work. From these short encounters you will gain a great deal of information.

85. Select your clothes carefully. You want your students to respect you as a teacher and identify you as the adult. Dress the part of a professional, and your students will see you as a professional.

86. Send a note to all of your students before classes begin, even high school students. Everyone loves to receive a personal message, but more importantly, you are making connections that can make a difference in a student's life.

87. If you are a teacher with a transition class (a class transferring from another building), pay special attention to the students in the hallway, at lunch, after school, and during class. Often they can be intimidated by the new surroundings and procedures. Make sure you let them know that you're available to answer any questions they may have.

88. Request students to write a short autobiography. Attach a picture of the student. You'll have an instant bulletin board display, which will help you to get to know the students. In addition, students will get to know each other.

89. Before you report for the first day of staff development in your district, utilize the Internet to help you find ideas, examples, and lessons that will tie into your curriculum. Take the ideas and use them to foster student growth.

90. Although you may have a well-planned lesson, you may have a few minutes left at the end of a class period. No matter what grade level, the unstructured time may turn into chaos. Create "fillers" or "sponge activities" that you can use just in case. When you haven't taught the material before, you will quite possibly overestimate or underestimate the time factor. Consider the following examples:

- An open-ended question about a topic you've been covering to be submitted when the bell rings
- A story problem that the students can turn to a partner and work on together
- "What if" questions that encourage critical thinking about the subject you've been covering

91. Think about how you will allocate the time the first day of class. Know what must be accomplished, and build your schedule accordingly. Think about the following:

- Greet students at the door with a smile (the students are very nervous and excited the first day).
- Take only a few minutes to tell the students about yourself.
- Take attendance orally (this may be the only time that you orally take attendance unless classes change every semester). This provides an opportunity to pronounce names and for students to correct you.
- Fill out forms and other necessary information provided by the office.

92. Prioritize what other things need to be accomplished on the first day. Depending on the time and the activity you have planned, you may need to do some of the following:

- Explain rules, guidelines, or expectations.
- Issue books (keep a master list of the book numbers and the person who is the "temporary tenant").
- If you have a fine arts room, science lab, or industrial tech room, you will want to provide a tour of the facilities. Reiterate safety issues as you tour.
- Give a short assignment either in class or for the next day. Get students back into school mode quickly.

93. If you are in an upper elementary or secondary classroom, provide each student with a colored index card. Ask students to write their first names in large letters followed by their last names in smaller letters underneath. Ask them to draw symbols that represent their interests and hobbies. On the backside of the card, ask the students to write their name, address, and phone number, plus the name of their parents or guardians, their address or phone number and email address (if they have one). You have now created a file of student names, addresses, and phone numbers. Each class can be a different color.

94. Watch or listen to the weather forecast every night. As a teacher you need to dress accordingly. Some buildings are not air-conditioned or climate controlled. Bring an extra change of clothing just in case someone spills on you, you spill on yourself, or the weather changes. If you teach younger students, you might want to incorporate weather tips as you instruct students how to dress the next day.

95. Anticipate what supplies you will need before school begins.

- Will you post a monthly list of birthdays? How will you remember every birthday?
- Will you be sending "good news notes" home? Address envelopes to every student.
- Design bulletin boards around themes, units, celebrations, and other concepts.

Preparing to Do It All over Again

96. Remember that learning doesn't stop at the end of the school year. Design a plan for the last few weeks of school that focuses on the following:

- A daily plan for achievement. It is easy to develop an attitude that learning doesn't matter anymore.
- Maintaining the same routines, expectations, and rules

- Encouraging students to stay on task, give their best effort, and work for quality
- Talking with your students, staying positive, and motivating your students to do their best until the last day

97. Communicate the following to your students during the last week:
- How much they have progressed
- Learning doesn't stop at the end of the school year
- The importance of continuing to read newspapers, magazines, books, and comic books
- How to recognize real-life math problems
- How science influences their everyday life
- You will miss them
- You hope that they will come back to visit next year

98. Make extra copies of handouts, worksheets, and practice sheets. Students misplace and lose papers and you will want to keep several in your files for next year. This will save you time running to make extra copies.

99. As you near the end of the school year, help students to reflect on the year by asking them to write about their favorite memory or experience in your class. Compile the remembrances in a class memory book to be distributed on the last day of school.

100. Write a personal letter to your students with a story, highlight, or accomplishment of the student that happened during the school year. Tell the student you enjoyed having him or her in class and that you wish them well next year.

101. During the last day of school, ask students to provide feedback as they reflect on the year. Have them write you a letter, answer a survey, or provide short answers to open-ended questions. Allow students to do this individually or in small groups.

102. Schedule an autograph party. If you have a school yearbook, you can have a yearbook signing party. As an alternative, you can have students make books where they can write personal messages to other students and sign their names. Model for the students the type of messages they can write in the books. If you have been taking digital pictures throughout the year, you can include several pages of class pictures.

103. If students are transitioning to another school, the end of the school year can heighten their anxieties about leaving their school for a different one. Help them to deal with their emotional stress by providing opportunities to talk about planning for next year. If the school does not have transition plans in place for students to visit the school or for the teachers to talk to the students, ask to set up a time to tour the school or invite the teachers to talk to the students. The more prepared students are for the new environment, the easier it will be for them next school year.

104. Have students write their names and addresses on postcards. During the summer take some time to write the students a short note about your summer and to ask about their summers. Take this opportunity to remind students to keep reading.

105. Near the end of the school year, design a letter writing lesson that will address the skills in letter writing by communicating with students in the grade above or below. Students will ask students in the grade above, questions about what to expect next year. Students will describe to students in the grade below their school year and offer suggestions for success.

106. Collect materials such as worksheets and book lists that students can take with them during the summer months. Include a map to the nearest library and a calendar with specific activities for every week.

107. For older students, provide a book list. Your media specialist or librarian can assemble a list of books to read that are appropriate for your students. Identify books by categories: recommend books for college, books for enjoyment, non-fiction books, and how-to books.

108. At the end of the school year, take time to organize and save your files on the computer. Delete any old emails, put documents into folders for filing, and trash unwanted items. Back up all necessary files on the server or on a disk. Generally over the summer, computers are cleaned and repaired as needed.

109. Also take time to organize your paper files. If you don't use it, toss it. Clear away all stacks of papers. Save, file, or toss. Place confidential files in secure places. This will save you time later and you won't be greeted by unfinished work when you return from the summer break.

110. Take an inventory of all the textbooks and reference books that you have in your room. Take home what you think you'll need to work on before returning in the weeks ahead.

111. Pack all materials and cover all the bookcases when school is out of session. The custodians will work to clean the rooms. You will want your materials to stay dust free.

112. Realize that you will go through the following six stages each year as a teacher:

- Anticipation—when you are so eager to get started
- Survival—where you can't seem to get ahead
- Disenchantment—when you question if you should stay in teaching
- Revitalization—when spring has arrived
- Reflection—when the year is nearly finished
- Anticipation—when you can't wait for school to start again

113. As you reflect on your school year, remember the people who helped you throughout the year. Send each of them a thank-you note for their assistance, compassion, and guidance. They will appreciate your thoughtfulness, and you will feel good about acknowledging very important gestures.

2.
Classroom Management

114. There are two main goals you have as a teacher at the beginning of the year. Cooperation and high achievement are your two expectations. You want your students to cooperate so they can learn and perform at their highest level of ability.

115. Create a classroom environment by developing a vision for your ideal working environment. It is easier to develop a classroom management plan if you have ideas and experiences to draw from. It will also be easier to come to work each day to a room that is functional as well as stimulating.

116. Frame the classroom management plan around a courteous, caring, respect-filled vision. Students who perceive that you care about them will perform better academically, are less likely to have behavior problems, and are more likely to be motivated. Take the vision, and fashion it into guidelines.

117. Keep your classroom management plan simple. Developing a complex management plan means that you will have to develop an elaborate record system with consequences. You only need to record absences, unexcused absences, and tardies.

118. Build a caring, trusting relationship with your students by talking to your students, taking interest in who they are and what they like, and listening to them. When positive relationships are in place it is much easier to resolve problems and maintain a good working relationship. Some students are very easy to like and connect with, but others may fray your nerves. Regardless, show all students that you care.

119. Before school begins in the morning, stand near your classroom door and greet students using their first names. This serves several purposes. First, you are personally welcoming students to class. Second, you can add a compliment or ask a quick question such as, "Great art show. I really liked your drawing..." or "Did you receive the message that I sent to you about..." Third, you may be the first adult who talks to them that morning. As the teacher you have just provided a short but meaningful interaction that tells students that they are a part of your class, and you are glad to see them.

120. Begin each day or class period with the same song, rap, or class response. An example might be:

Teacher: *Are you ready?*

Students: *Yes, we're ready.*

Teacher: *Ready for what?*

Students: *Ready to learn.*

Together: *Let's learn!*

Each class can make up the opening for the day. It is said in a loud voice with great enthusiasm. When students respond together, they find their voice and are more apt to participate in class. This promotes positive feelings and excitement.

121. Periodically vary the class response, choral response, rap, or song to fit the theme for the day or the unit. The change will draw attention to a new unit, theme, or to a special occasion. A group response sends the message of unison and brings an emotional connection.

122. End each day or period by asking each student as they walk out the door to respond to an unfinished statement such as, "I learned...", "I would change...", or "I didn't understand..." You gain a better understanding of individual student's thoughts, and students have a voice to share in private, which further builds a sense of belonging.

123. Initiate activities and unique experiences in your classroom that build traditions. Students talk about the activities and look forward to being in the classroom because they are a part of a tradition that promotes positive feelings and a sense of pride. For example, create a "Wall of Pride" where pictures of students are posted because they met a challenge in the classroom. Each year more teams of students are added. In kindergarten, students could celebrate 100 days of school by bringing one hundred items to school. In sixth grade, all students could be involved in a medieval parade through the halls before the end of the unit. In tenth grade, students could participate in a Civil War reenactment. Students will remember and talk about these experiences for years.

124. Remember that everything you do in the classroom—tone of voice, facial expression, body movements, and stance—sends a message to students. When you call a student by his or her first name, respond with a "please" and "thank you," or greet students with a smile, you immediately send a positive message that this is a friendly, inviting environment.

125. Keep a current list (paper copy) of your students, parent/guardian names, addresses, and phone numbers. Place the list in a bright envelope, in a drawer, or cabinet for easy access in case of a fire or natural disaster. You are responsible for your group of students. If you need a quick role call, you will have names in hand. If you have to call parents, you have all the information.

126. Ask students to bring only their books, pencils/pens, and paper to class to maximize space. If students bring their backpacks, find a place away from the teaching area to place them during class. Cluttered rooms can cause students to trip or become frustrated. You need to rearrange the room or provide students with a space for their possessions.

Arrange with Easy Management in Mind

127. As you begin the school year and get to know your students, place the students who need more space to move to the sides of the seating arrangement. Give them an aisle on the outside to be able to utilize the space for stretching and moving uninhibitedly. Some of your more rambunctious students need more space, which the outside aisles will provide.

128. Purposefully arrange desks or tables to accommodate learning and minimize misbehavior. Your arrangements need to facilitate various activities and keep disruptive behavior to a minimum. When students become frustrated with visual or physical barriers in their way, they will begin to act out inappropriately. Consider the following arrangements and the purpose for the placement:

- Rows for short lectures or testing
- Large circle for sharing and discussing as a whole group
- Desks/tables for small group discussion and cooperative learning
- Semi-circle for presentations

129. Based on the lesson and the delivery, a seating arrangement should never be permanent and can change with the way the lesson is presented. When changing seating arrangements, designate where students will sit before class begins. Use an overhead to assign seats. As the students walk into the room, have them check where they need to sit or orchestrate the change yourself quickly, preserving class time for academic instruction.

130. Arrange the classroom so that it allows for easy flow of traffic. With any age group, a slight push, trip, or bump might cause some pushing or shoving. Be proactive by arranging the tables or desks with enough space for students to walk easily and freely. This will minimize classroom management issues.

131. Place yourself in an area where you can reach all students and where you can see all students. You need to be able to make eye contact with all of your students as a form of communication, and you need to be able to reach all students quickly if they need help or need to be disciplined.

132. Locate your desk outside of the main teaching area. Effective teachers don't teach from behind their desk. Consider moving the desk to the back of the room instead of the front to create an area where students can conference one-on-one with you in a more private area. This also gives you a good vantage point to supervise students at work.

133. Keep the classroom tidy and organized. Avoid unnecessary clutter that will distract from instruction, inhibit the flow of traffic, or cause you to take time to look for a misplaced item. Students are thrown off task quickly, so alleviate natural or physical barriers as much as possible.

Set Rules Early and Stick to Them

134. Model the guidelines that either you or you and your class have established. If you believe that being on time, being prepared, and being an active listener are important, then model these behaviors for your students. Begin the class on time, be organized, and listen when students are responding to you. Your actions show students that you also believe in the guidelines for the class.

135. Spend time introducing classroom rules by explaining, modeling, and practicing the rules. Students need to gain an understanding of the rules by practicing until the rules become routine. For example, students need to practice lining up for recess, walking to an assembly, waiting for the teacher to dismiss them, and asking for help. Classroom misbehavior is less likely to occur when the students know what the rules are and how they need to act.

136. If rules are broadly stated, take time to make the rules concrete by asking students what "Be respectful" looks like, feels like, and sounds like. Do the same with "Be a thinker" or "Be prepared." Students need to translate the words into observable actions, words, and feelings in order to understand what is expected.

137. State rules positively to show students how to behave instead of stating how not to behave. A negative indicates that students are doing something wrong.

138. Keep the number of rules short. Teachers and students won't be able to remember more than five rules. If no one can remember the rules, how can they follow the rules?

139. When establishing rules, develop the consequences that will result if the rule is not followed. Hold students accountable for their behavior with consistent consequences. If you are not consistent, you lose your credibility and students will try to "beat the system."

140. When appropriate, involve students in establishing rules. Some teachers find that students who are involved in making the rules are less likely to violate them because of their ownership in crafting the rules.

141. Post the rules of the classroom on the wall near the designated area where you will talk to students who misbehave. You can refer to the rules as you are talking to students because reminders redirect behavior in a positive way.

142. Send a copy of the rules home with students with a section for parents/guardians and students to sign that they agree and will abide by the established rules. Ask students to review with the parents/guardians and bring the signed copy back. Keep it on file in case you need to remind students that they agreed to follow the rules. Students will have little retort after the reminder.

143. Place a "brag box" in your room and have students write on a piece of paper when they see teachers or students doing good things. Randomly read the brag notes to the class to reinforce good behavior.

Procedures, Routines, and Expectations Are Important

144. Establish procedures for conducting the class. Procedures explain behaviors associated with certain tasks such as how to enter the room, how to get supplies, or how to get into groups. Procedures keep the classroom running smoothly and safely. Practicing turns the procedures into routines.

145. Make a list of procedures before school begins that you need to explain, demonstrate, and practice. Plan how and when you will introduce each procedure. Examples of procedures include:
• How to enter the room
• How to leave the class
• How and where to get supplies
• Where to put completed assignments

146. Establish your own procedures as the teacher. Procedures for everyday tasks help to structure a student's day and the teacher's day by keeping the class running smoothly. The following are examples to consider when instituting procedures: Taking attendance, keeping a daily log, documenting student misbehavior, taking lunch count, and collecting money.

147. When role-playing behavior expectations, have an adult act out the inappropriate behavior and the student act out the expected behavior. You do not want to reinforce inappropriate behavior by allowing the student to perform that role.

148. Help students that do not feel like they fit in and act out for peer attention and approval. Viewing short film clips of social situations will assist students in a discussion about appropriate and inappropriate behavior.

149. Periodically hold classroom meetings to address issues within the classroom, explain a new procedure, or develop plans for a service project. Give students a way to express themselves, problem solve, and support each other.

150. Preserve precious class time by insisting students be on time for class. If a teacher only has forty minutes of prime instructional time, every minute does count. Students arriving late cause disruptions in the flow of the lesson.

151. If students are not on time, do not send them for a pass from the office. Too much time is wasted. Hold students responsible. Have a policy in place that states students will make up the time either early in the morning, after school, or during recess. If students don't show for the "make-up" time, provide one more chance, but adding more time. If they don't show, allow the principal or the dean of students to handle the situation.

152. If you are having a problem with tardy students, write an extra credit question on the board to be answered the first three minutes of class. If the student is not in his or her seat when the bell rings, he or she will not be able to receive extra credit. If you don't believe in giving extra credit, the question or problem could be for regular credit.

153. Due dates for assignments instill timelines and a sense of responsibility for the student. If the students struggle with a sense of deadlines and time, help them organize their priorities and set expectations for on-time delivery. Post due dates on board and check to make sure students write dates in their planners.

154. The chronic "late assignment student" will need to conference with you about an agreed upon deadline. A simple one-page contract between the teacher and the student should state the expectation and why it is late. The two of you should come to an agreement of action to resolve the lateness. Be sure to document the meeting. If the late assignments persist, contact the parents/guardians.

155. Teach social skills on a daily basis in elementary school. Use cooperative learning to teach social skills at the middle school and high school level. Younger students need to learn how to address other teachers, how to move quickly and quietly, and how to use first names. Older students need to learn how to be active listeners, use quiet voices, and ask for clarification.

156. Begin to generate a timeline of major concepts covered. Continue to add concepts as studied. This provides a visual reference and a continuum of learning that helps students remember and make connections.

157. Individual behavior plans provide the framework to assist students with a plan to change behavior. Focus on the positive and on reinforcement. Consequences are the last issue you discuss when writing a plan with the student, teacher, and family. Do not use negative consequences that will humiliate the student. Keep in mind the dignity of the person.

158. Students should be aware of what the consequences are if they misbehave or do not complete their assignments. Visit with your colleagues to be assured the consequences in your classroom match school-wide consequences. The consequence should always fit the situation.

159. Teach students that respect also means respect for the support staff, custodians, cooks, and bus drivers. Students forget sometimes that we are all members of a school community. Respect is for everyone.

160. Teach students what the expectations are for extracurricular activities and sporting events. Students need to be taught how they are to act outside of the classroom; don't assume that they know or have been taught at home.

161. Explain to your students what academic dishonesty is and is not. They also need to know the policy and consequences regarding it. Make sure that you have evidence and not assumptions when you address a student's integrity. If all proves to be true, follow your procedures. Don't ever make a mockery of a student in front of peers.

Conflict and Behavior Management

162. Be aware that your class will consist of many actors and actresses. You will have the drama queen who thinks every moment is a crisis for her. You will have the class clown who will try to draw attention to his or her clever antics and one-liners. And the list can go on. Don't feed the personalities. Focus on their strengths, and at the same time deal with any behavior that may disrupt the learning in the classroom.

163. Designate an area where you can confer with students about their behavior outside of the main instruction area. If you need to respond to misbehavior, take the student to this area to minimize disruption to the other students. Never turn your back to the class when talking one-on-one with a student in the area designated for feedback.

164. As you talk with students about their behavior problems, stand in one spot and talk in a quiet, deliberate voice. Make direct eye contact. Refrain from touching the student or poking them when you want to make a point. Generally when students are pulled aside for a behavior management session, the teacher is upset or angry with the student. If this comes across in the conference, it only will escalate the situation.

165. If conflicts arise amongst the students in the classroom, or are carried into the classroom from outside, use conflict resolution to help students resolve the matter with a structured protocol. Ask the guidance counselor about a training session that you can attend. Gaining knowledge in this area will help you throughout your career.

166. Be aware of harassment and bullying issues in the classroom or in the hallway. Find the harassment policy in the student handbook or the district's policy book. Read the policy to the students and talk about what this means and the implications for those who do not follow the policy.

167. When dealing with tough, highly-charged, confrontational situations, remain calm and maintain control. If students see you as vulnerable, they will not stop their tirade. If you become agitated, take charge of your emotions quickly before the conflict between you and the student escalates.

168. Address behavior that violates school policy head-on. Turning your head or covering your ears only shows that you don't care about the school rules. Find out the name of the student if you don't know his or her name. Write a note to the office explaining the misbehavior. The principal or dean of students will follow up with the referral.

169. In the classroom, in the hallways, and in other areas of the school building and grounds, keep your eyes moving. A quick glance might stop potential misbehaviors from happening. This is a quick way to stop actions a student might regret later. If you witness an infraction, address it personally with the student, or report the infraction to the office.

170. Establish a graduated system for addressing misbehavior within the classroom for such actions as not paying attention, writing notes, sleeping, or blurting out of turn. Consider the following consequences as examples for not following the rules:

1st offense: Address the misbehavior

2nd offense: Give a detention or time out

3rd offense: Double the detention, and request a conference with the student

4th offense: Call parents/guardians

5th offense: Send to the office and meet with the parents/guardians

Other interventions to consider might be include writing a management contract for the student, and creating a discipline plan or a behavior modification plan.

171. When contacting parents, script what you plan to say to them about their child's behavior in the classroom. It can be intimidating to talk to parents for the first time on the telephone. End the conversation by telling parents to call or email you at school when they have questions or concerns.

172. Use office referrals as the last way of dealing with student behavior. Ask yourself if you have tried all possibilities. Alert the principal that you have addressed a student's misbehavior and inform them of the steps that you have taken to remediate the situation.

173. When writing behavior contracts, ask for student input because you will have more of a buy-in from the student. Carefully craft the wording to reflect the actions that the student must follow. Send a copy to the parents so that they are aware of what is happening.

174. Think twice about giving frequent rewards for good behavior. This is an expectation not a celebration, and sends the message that they did something exceptional when they did exactly as expected. Save the stickers, candy, and other treats for special occasions.

175. Recognize students for positive behavior by sending them notes that highlight their positive contributions. This will reinforce their behavior and contribute to the positive environment.

176. Utilize nonverbal cues to send messages to students to stop misbehaving and refocus. Keep an eye on the student until the student resumes appropriate behavior. Using nonverbal cues does not interfere with the flow of a lesson, but it does send a quick message to the student.

177. If a knowing glance is not enough, approach a student who continues to stay off task. When students catch the direct eye contact as you are moving toward them, they will get back on task. These movements tell the student that his or her behavior was unacceptable.

178. Use gestures to communicate with students that they need to get back on task. A simple signal is worth many words if you train your students to respond to the gesture. No yelling, gnashing of teeth, or screaming is necessary. Teach the gesture to all of the students, practice, and then implement. For example:

- Tap quietly on the student's desk to let him or her know that the student is off task.
- Use thumbs up to reinforce a positive behavior; use thumbs to the side to provide a warning that a student is close to misbehaving; use thumbs down to indicate that the behavior needs to stop.
- Tap on your watch. This is a signal that students are wasting time and that they need to get back on task.

179. Acknowledge with a quiet thank you when students stop the misbehavior. It shows that you recognize that they have stopped the inappropriate actions and are refocused again.

180. Use gestures to encourage good behavior. Teach the entire class how you plan to gain their attention. Using these methods, you don't have to shout to get students' attention. Practice using one of these ways to gain students' attention:

- Clap three times if you want silence. They, in turn, clap three times back. Then you have their attention.
- Use a whistle or a bell to get their attention.
- Place your hand in the air, palm facing the students. Count to three by putting one, two, and then three fingers down.

181. Refrain from arguing with a student. This is a lose/lose situation. When you find yourself responding with several points, drop the linguistics, and repeat what you expect the student to do. If they continue to argue, provide the student with a choice to argue after school or focus on his or her schoolwork.

182. Provide students with choices when addressing behavior problems. The student has some control over the outcome of the discussion. For example, ask the student if he or she plans to finish the work now, during lunch, or after school. Ask the student if he or she plans to pay attention now or after school.

183. Avoid using idle threats, punishments, or other punitive tactics. This degrades not only students, but also reflects negatively on you. Refer to the classroom rules and the consequences established, and follow through appropriately.

184. Work with students on a daily basis to establish positive character traits that exemplify qualities that students will need to model both in and out of school. These include responsibility, honesty, and trust.

185. Be careful about making assumptions about students. If you didn't observe a student misbehaving, don't make assumptions about who you think was in the wrong.

186. Apologize if you wrongly accused a student, if you became angry, or if you were short with students. Express your regret. Students will appreciate your honesty.

187. Avoid leaving the classroom. Send a student or call the office if you need an item, assistance, or help. The class is your responsibility. An unattended classroom invites misbehavior by the students, unexpected accidents, or bullying and harassment. You will be held liable for any negative actions that occur during your absence.

188. If you must leave the room in an emergency situation, call the office on the intercom; tell the students this is an emergency situation and that you need their cooperation. Students should realize how to behave during serious moments and will most likely be responsible for their actions for a few minutes.

189. Learn how to determine what needs your immediate attention and what can be dealt with at another time individually or in a class meeting. If a student is in danger, if there is a physical altercation, or if a student uses profanity, address the behavior immediately. If a student rolls their eyes, gives a sigh, or mutters his or her disdain, address the situation later in a quiet manner.

190. Don't overreact to minor infractions. Problems generally escalate when a teacher loses control. Take several deep breaths, and plan what you want to say and do next using a firm but quiet voice.

191. Do not reprimand a student publicly unless his or her safety or someone else's safety is in jeopardy. A quick, quiet, and firm reprimand will have a better impact on the student's behavior and self-esteem.

192. If you witness a fight in the school or on the grounds, send a student to the office to get the principal. Firmly and in a loud voice, tell the students to stop immediately. Refrain from grabbing the students because you might get pulled into the fight. If the command does not stop the fight, repeat the message to stop. Get other students out of the way. If the fight stops before assistance arrives, escort the students to the office.

193. When a student damages school property, direct the student to make restitution, repair the item in question, and apologize. Students need to be held accountable for their actions. The consequence needs to fit the action taken.

194. When a student arrives for a detention in your room, use the time to catch-up on missing assignments, talk with the student, or work together on the day's work. If the detention time is not structured, students will sit and do nothing. Use the time to optimize learning by structuring the student's time with you.

195. Remember the following: Never give an entire class a detention. The fewer students in detention, the easier it will be to focus on individual problems and solutions and to clarify any misunderstandings before they manifest and become major conflicts.

196. Constantly review the way that you are dealing with misbehavior in the classroom. Analyze your beliefs about classroom management, your teaching style, and organization. Think about ways that you might be contributing to the misbehavior and how you might rectify this. You may have too strict of a management plan or be too liberal when dealing with student misbehavior. You may not have an engaging lesson. Or you may be too scattered in your thoughts or in your lesson flow.

197. If a student continues to misbehave in your classroom, schedule a conference with the student to gain more information and focus on possible solutions. Ask the student to pinpoint the problem. When the problem is identified and agreed upon by both of you, begin to explore ways to address the misbehavior. Find a solution that you both can agree upon. Schedule a time to get back together to ascertain how things are going.

198. Carefully document misbehavior. Develop a record keeping system that works for you whether it is note cards or a computer program. You simply can't remember every infraction and consequence given. Keep the records current. The principal or guidance counselor may ask you about previous misbehavior. You can email or make a copy of your records, complete with dates and consequences.

199. If a parent-teacher meeting is needed and the student is denying any link to misbehavior, contact the dean of students, the counselor, the principal, or another teacher to be present at the conference. The first few parent-teacher conferences can be intimidating. The presence of another adult can be very supportive and helpful in seeking solutions.

200. Keep all information confidential. You need to act professionally and show respect for the student and parents. Do not comment on a troubled student's behavior to other students.

201. During the meeting with parents, be careful how you state the misbehavior that occurred in class. Consider asking the student about his or her perceptions about an incident or series of occurrences. This gives students some power and control at the meeting. Continue to ask appropriate, non-threatening questions that direct the student to think about the negative behavior.

202. If student behavior improves, do not hesitate to send a note to the student, their parents, and the principal. This positive communication is needed to build effective relationships with students.

203. Contact the school counselor or administration about resources that can lend support and direction and are available to students and parents. Does the school district have a social worker assigned, an at-risk coordinator, or a police liaison to help students who have problems?

204. Know what agencies, organizations, and other resources are available in your region that might be of help to you. Before you contact any outside resources, contact the school counselor or the administration. Provide the name of a support agency only as a possible solution to the problem the student is exhibiting. You are not a counselor so tread carefully when suggesting specific outside resources.

205. Understand that some students are required to meet with outside agency personnel as part of a program. You may be asked to provide input about a student's behavior or attend a meeting after school to report on the student's behavior and academic progress. Bring documentation to the meeting about behavior and updated grades.

206. Be aware that some students are adjudicated and require a tracker (a person who is assigned by the courts to be a contact for a student throughout the day and night) to check in with before and after school. Unless you have been contacted by the office, do not let a student leave the classroom to call his or her tracker. All phone calls should be made after class. However, if students must meet with their court appointed contact during your class, remember that your lesson at that time may not be a priority in the student's life.

207. Periodically develop a paper or electronic survey where your class responds to classroom management issues. They will appreciate the opportunity to provide their feedback, and it will give you another perspective.

208. If you are having difficulty with a particular student, find the school counselor who is trained to provide guidance. They are generally good listeners, and sometimes you may need an objective person who can buffer your emotions during a particularly challenging day. It is healthy to vent your feelings in a safe environment.

209. Remember that you are a mandatory reporter of abuse. If you believe that a child has been abused (visible marks, bruises, verbal acknowledgement, change in behavior), make a note and observe the student until you can talk with a school counselor, principal, or school nurse. Your first step is to contact the counselor, the nurse, or the principal. They will generally handle the report but you may have to verify what you know about the situation.

210. Don't make a big production of students writing notes, but address it privately by confiscating all notes. Stop it when it first happens, not after the fifth time.

211. Develop a policy and punishment routine for the use of electronic devices in the classroom such as Game Boys, pagers, cell phones, and cell phones with cameras. Most schools have a policy that restricts the use of electronic devices. Rehearse beforehand how you will deal with the problem during class when you discover a student text messaging or playing a game.

212. When dealing with a misbehaving student, do not stop the class and call attention to the behavior. Move toward the student and quietly tell the student that you will need to see him or her after class about the infraction.

213. Periodically, assess your classroom management plan. What needs to be tweaked? What is working well? Unless students are out of control, don't change the plan. It is difficult for students to adjust.

3.

Developing Lessons

214. Allow plenty of time to develop your lesson plans. When you are designing a lesson, you are taking content and developing strategies to effectively reach your students. Designing a lesson takes planning, creativity, and knowledge of your material.

215. Decide at the beginning of the school year what critical thinking skills you want your students to acquire by the end of the school year. By making a conscious effort at identifying these skills and making this a goal, you are more apt to incorporate them in your curriculum.

216. Ask a teacher in your school where to find the standards and benchmarks for your subject or grade level. Next, find any sample lessons or units that the previous teacher kept. Take time to peruse the information that has been acquired. This will be very helpful when you structure your own lesson plans.

217. Use butcher paper to sketch out the entire semester or year. You will be able to see how all of the units and supporting material fit together. When you begin a unit, you need to know the bigger picture and how it all fits together. This big-picture perspective will help you develop your lesson plans for the entire year.

218. Clearly state what students are expected to accomplish during each lesson by including a specific statement of the learning. As you are writing a lesson, the objectives will guide you.

219. As you work with the unit organizer, how will you know that students have mastered the material? What form of assessment will you design? Does the assessment align with the lesson? If you ask your students to put together a motor, you shouldn't give them a multiple choice test. Putting the motor together itself illustrates their competency at the task.

220. Have clear and specific academic expectations for your students. Communicate them to your students, their families, and the school administration. Explain to the various parties how you plan to help students meet these expectations.

221. As soon as you determine what materials students will need, take the worksheets, activity sheets, articles, directions, quizzes, and tests to the copy machine and submit a work order. Understand that running multiple copies for multiple teachers takes time. If you don't give the person who makes copies a few days notice, you may find yourself without a test.

222. Plan and teach with the end in mind. As you are teaching, check with yourself to see if you are still on the path to what you want the students to know and be able to do when they finish the unit. An easy filter to use when making lesson plans are the following:

- Keep essential, basic information
- Place ideas or supplemental information you think you will use in a separate file
- Discard information or ideas that you know will cause you or the class to stray from the main lesson

223. It is difficult to know what is important for students when you begin a new unit, class, or course you haven't taught before. Refer back to the unit organizer that you drew and reassess what is important. Have you covered all of the areas you flagged as essential?

224. Be purposeful when constructing lessons. Make the content more meaningful to the students by telling them why each lesson is important.

225. Refrain from getting stuck in classroom discussions about trivial information. Clearly analyze each lesson to focus on the most important concepts. As an educator, think about what information will serve your students best in the long run, and make that a priority.

226. Be creative when preparing your lessons. This may sound easy to do, but it takes a great deal of thought. Talk to other teachers about how you plan to develop a lesson. Generally they will offer other ideas about how they designed their lessons. Good ideas and feedback will generate new ideas.

227. Think carefully about the questions you will be asking during class time. You may want to include questions that relate to Bloom's Taxonomy, which helps you assess what is required from the type of questions you are asking (i.e., asking a question that requires knowledge necessitates that the student has memorized information).:

Knowledge	• Requires memorization
Comprehension	• Requires rewording of information
Application	• Requires applying knowledge to figure out an answer
Analysis	• Recognizes causes • Draws conclusions • Determines evidence
Synthesis	• Makes predictions • Combines elements to produce original product • Solves problems with more than one possible answer
Evaluation	• Makes judgments • Offers opinions

Purposefully plan questions that cause students to think (analysis, synthesis, evaluation).

228. Create lessons that allow your students time in class to work on a new skill by providing a short period of time to work on sample problems, set up a lab, read a passage, or sew a button hole. You will be able to guide students as they practice the new skill. If students have questions, you are able to help. Use following technique: "I do" (the teacher models the skill), "we do" (the teacher and students practice the skill together), and "you do" (the students work alone on the skill).

229. Give students choices during a lesson. You can provide a list of supplemental activities for the students to do, such as novels to read, experiments to do, or projects to complete. Students feel empowered and more in control of their learning.

230. Integrate subjects as you plan units. Show students that learning is not isolated. Read a historical novel while studying history. While studying math, bring in a science problem. Students don't always correlate why you need to study science in English class. You need to show them why this is important.

231. Provide opportunities for students to reflect on their learning. This provides a time out for students to think about not only what they learned, but how they learn best. You can use journals, note cards, a structured response worksheet, or a verbal response. Collect the students' thoughts and use them to ascertain if they are learning the material.

232. As a part of a lesson, take time for the class to write either a whole group thank-you note, a committee thank-you note, or individual thank-you notes. Students of all ages need the practice in composing thank-you notes and addressing an envelope. You will need to proofread the letters before they are sent. The recipients love to read the notes. This is another way the school connects with the community.

233. When planning a lesson, schedule time for debate and discussion, rather than lecturing all the time. Let the students develop solutions to questions through critical thinking and discussions with their peers.

234. Use a three-ring binder, a file cabinet, or your computer to keep all of the materials used for each lesson together. This will keep you organized and you will be able to access information quickly when you want to work on it. Keep all materials labeled. It will be much easier for you to find the following year when you redesign the unit and use the materials again.

235. Begin organizing the lessons by developing piles of materials that will supplement the content. Keep the lesson-planning process ongoing so that you don't find yourself without a plan for the next day.

236. For quick drills that require short answers, use individual white boards. The students can quickly hold them up and you can see who understands and who doesn't understand. Check to see if the school will purchase the large sheets and then check to see if one of the custodians or buildings and grounds keeper could cut these for your students.

237. Use ways to tap students' prior knowledge of a subject before designing a unit. You will be able to determine how you will address the diversity of thinking among your students. Simply ask students what they know about a subject and what they want to know about a subject.

238. Provide closure to a lesson by asking the students to provide a quick three sentence summary before the bell rings. You can do this as a group or individually.

239. When planning a short discussion time, ask students to write their thoughts about the topic before verbalizing them. Students will be more articulate because they have thought about the question twice. Give students enough time to think about their answers. Encourage the students who finish early to dig deeper and add to their answer.

240. Think about the time of day when you teach students. The first period of the day, after lunch, and the last period of the day can offer some challenging behavior such as feeling lethargic in the morning, sleepy or hyper after lunch, and energetic during the last period of the day. Vary your teaching strategy to address student needs based on the time of day.

241. Don't assume that students know how to use study skills. You will need to plan lessons that teach students how to study. Provide them with the tips that they need to be successful learners. Teach the skill, model, and practice until the student makes this a part of an automatic routine.

242. Use questions in your lessons to help students make inferences. The majority of standardized test questions are inferential, and the majority of students need practice using inferences to find answers.

243. Many quick and easy ideas for the classroom can be found perusing the books in the bookstore. Take time to browse the education section and skim any books that pertain to your subject or grade level.

244. Use nonfiction books to augment your curriculum. Go to the media center to find titles that correspond with the curriculum. Use them for direct instruction, for supplementary use, or to display. Students need to understand that their textbook is not the only source for information.

245. Ask other teachers who have taught the course to help you plan the class or provide you with direction. Teachers are very willing to share their knowledge, materials, and expertise. Don't be afraid to ask.

246. Think about how you want to begin the lesson. You might consider using a short anecdote, a question, a dramatic moment, or a song that will grab students' attention and get their minds engaged on the learning that is taking place.

247. When designing the end of your lesson plan, ask students to develop questions for a test, quiz, or for a review. A good strategy to teach students is the Question-Answer Relationship. Through this strategy designed by Taffy E. Raphael, students think about the type of question they are formulating. Students learn about four types of questions:

- Right There: The questions can be found in one area in the text. These are literal-level questions.
- Think and Search: Students have to review several areas of the text to generate an answer. These are inferential questions.
- Author and Me: The answer is not in the text. The student needs to know what the author says and combine that information with the student's knowledge.
- On My Own: The answer relies on prior knowledge and may not have to read to answer the question.

248. Using fiction or non-fiction literature to supplement your textbook content will increase the meaningfulness of the subject matter and broaden students' knowledge of the subject. Be sure to include outside sources to use when preparing your lesson plan.

249. Place vocabulary words and definitions on the board or on the wall for students to review throughout the week. Use the words in conversation during the week. Don't give more than five words per week. After testing the students at the end of the week, review throughout the year. Students will have a greater chance of retaining the vocabulary words.

Be Clear about Objectives and Expectations

250. If you are a high school teacher consider writing a syllabus for your class. Include student objectives, assignments, a calendar, and other pertinent information. This general plan will help you to plan the course and will help students understand what is expected of them. This will also give them a sneak peek at what to expect in college.

251. Give clear expectations for homework assignments. State the purpose of the homework, why it is important, and what you hope the student will learn from it. If you believe that a student needs additional practice, tell the student and the parents. Be sure to communicate exactly how much time you think it should take to complete each assignment.

252. Post the content area standards and benchmarks in the classroom on a large, laminated poster. Refer to the standards and benchmarks when you are teaching. Students need to understand what standards they need to achieve in each of their classes.

253. State daily lesson and unit objectives and write them on the board every day. Students need to see and hear what is being expected of them. Objectives are their road map to learning. At the end of the unit, refer back to the objectives and ask students if the objectives were met. Ask them to support their answers by providing their reasoning.

254. During a lesson, model for students what you expect them to produce. Provide students with a clear and concise step-by-step procedure that they will understand. Think aloud as you model for students. Often teachers give an assignment without communicating to students how to accomplish the task. It is easier for students to understand the task if they can see and hear your demonstration.

255. During a lesson, make sure you check in with your students to ensure that they understand what is being taught. You can obtain a quick perspective of who gets it and who needs more instruction or practice by asking some simple questions about the topic you are studying.

256. Know that students need to have a variety of activities, as well as structure, clear directions, and expectations for the activity. Reiteration of the classroom rules from time to time is also appropriate.

257. Teach students how to respond to a question by setting the following guidelines:

- Raise your hand or wait until someone else has finished talking.
- Raise your hand enough for the teacher to see. Waving and jumping out of your seat is distracting to others. Wait patiently.
- Listen to what others have to say because they may answer your question.

258. Teach students to take notes. Students will try to record everything that they hear. Give them strategies that will help them to identify the most important things.

259. Teach students how to set goals. Long-range goals can be set for the school year. Short-term goals can be set for each unit. Take the time to incrementally look at where the students perceive themselves in terms of meeting the goals.

260. Teach students how to summarize information. They need to know how to effectively restate information in their own words. Students generally will copy a passage word for word and call it summarizing. Show students how to highlight the major points of a passage.

261. Ask students to make predictions about what will happen next in a passage, in an experiment, or in a video clip. You will test students' assumptions about what they are reading.

262. When learning vocabulary words, find student-friendly definitions. Ask students to draw a visual representation of the word and to make up a story that will help them to remember the word.

263. Take the time, early in the year, to help students understand textbook structures. Don't waste time by focusing on unimportant things.

264. Instruct students to always have their schedules in their planners and with them all day. Keeping their schedules with them teaches them to be organized and also ensures they know exactly when assignments are due.

Supplement Your Lessons

265. After you have sketched out the units, add supplemental materials, activities, speakers, films, and other events that you think will align with the learning. You will have planned an entire course and included an easy to follow guide. Make sure that when you make your schedule, you're planning according to your school's calendar.

266. Think carefully about sticking to a textbook. Learning isn't about covering the entire text, but rather about digging deep into the content. You may find that you are running a race to cover all the material instead of following a focused plan.

267. Consider speakers who can add another voice of experience to supplement the content. Meet with the speaker ahead of time to compare notes so that they will support and align with what you have taught.

268. After you have mapped out the unit and listed supplemental materials, find the materials you need for a unit, call speakers, order films, and develop learning strategies. How the information is presented is sometimes more important than the content.

269. As you design lessons, work with the media specialist in your building. The school's media resources can supplement units and provide students with a variety of print and software material.

270. Ask questions before a video, performance, demonstration, or reading. When you ask questions, students begin to focus on the learning opportunity. Asking a higher category of questions will focus the student and require a thought process to begin to take shape before the learning experience takes place.

Plan for All Students

271. As you are designing lessons, ask yourself how you will address the needs of each individual student. Accommodate the learning styles of your students by presenting a variety of challenging opportunities in your classroom. One size does not fit all in classrooms today.

272. Include ways to actively involve students in the learning process by incorporating interactive strategies in the lesson. Allow students to develop their own ideas, independent of yours. Have a debate, role play, or have students spend time sharing with a partner.

273. Improve student learning by allowing students to find areas of interest to them. Reread the student interest surveys collected at the beginning of the school year. You may find some common interests among small groups of students. Develop lessons that incorporate those interests.

274. On a daily basis make notes about what went well in your lesson and what needs to be changed. If you don't make these notations, you will forget what you intended to change. Keep these notes either in your planner or attached to the unit. You can refer back to these notes when planning next year's lessons.

275. Remember that a student's attention span matches his or her age. Ask speakers to speak for a specified time and then insert a time for the students to partner with a classmate and write a question to ask the speaker. Collect the questions and give them to the speaker. The speaker can decide which ones to answer. Using a more structured way of asking questions causes students to think about what they will ask instead of blurting out questions or remaining silent.

276. Remember that some students will be reading at a much lower level than others. Some students who have low reading scores are receiving special education and some are not. You need to know this information as you plan lessons.

277. When designing lessons, match the content with developmentally appropriate activities. If activities are too childish for a grade level, students will not be challenged to participate. If an activity is too difficult, students will become frustrated and little learning will occur.

278. Design activities that will stretch students' thinking; don't design activities that are all fun and no learning. Students' time in schools must be maximized with meaningful learning experiences. Careful planning is key. Playing a hang man game or doing a word search needs to be replaced by students designing their own games, or by a fun vocabulary strategy that ties into the standards and benchmark of the district.

279. Consider students' learning styles when designing lesson plans. Add opportunities for the tactile, kinesthetic, auditory, and visual learner. Design activities that foster learning using these styles. Make sure that you continue to rotate each style so that you can connect with all of the students.

Informal Groups

280. Learning occurs through social interaction. Utilizing groups in lesson design helps to foster more effective and meaningful interaction. Groups can stay together throughout a unit, for a week, or a lesson for a few minutes depending on your purpose.

281. Use a variety of grouping practices in the classroom. Keep the groups flexible depending on your purpose. Know what your goal is and assign groups accordingly. Do not allow students to group themselves. If you know you're going to do a group project, plan the groups the day before.

282. If you use small groups or if students are working on many class projects, find a device that will get their attention if you need to make an announcement or give additional directives. Devices may be wands, timers, bells, or whistles. Have students practice what they need to do when you use one of the devices.

283. When using groups to facilitate learning, assign the groups yourself. This gives you the opportunity to pair students according to their learning style or knowledge level so they can learn from one another.

284. Keep the size of groups small—generally from two to five students. This gives each student an opportunity for interaction.

285. Encourage group interaction and completion of the task. Never sit at your desk when groups are meeting. Listen to what they are saying as you rotate around the room.

286. Periodically ask a group to present their information to another group. This will hold the students accountable for their learning.

Formal Cooperative Learning

287. Remember that cooperative learning produces greater achievement than more conventional methods. The development of social skills is an added benefit. If you have not been trained in cooperative learning, think about enrolling in a course or attending a staff development session to enhance your skills.

288. Cooperative learning is more than placing students into groups. It is about purposefully planning a lesson that intentionally uses small groups. Cooperative learning is an effective way of building communities of learners, providing peer support, teaching social skills, and working together to solve problems or produce a product.

289. When designing a cooperative learning lesson, planning is the key to a successful learning experience. The reason to use cooperative learning is to encourage everyone to work together to the best of their ability to achieve a goal. Using cooperative learning groups helps to build a more purposeful structure for students.

290. Design groups based on your purpose. You want a cross section of students in each group. Begin to build the "all for one and one for all" belief by telling students that they are in this group to help each other succeed.

291. When specifically using cooperative learning you need to assign groups of three to five students each with a specific role. If you have more than five it is difficult to find a specific role for each student. Each person in the group needs a task. Roles can be the leader, the recorder, the observer, the reporter, the task master, the activity director, and the process observer. Cooperative groups must have assigned roles.

292. In a cooperative learning lesson, the following social skills can be taught and modeled by the teacher:
- Using first names
- Moving quickly and quietly
- Offering encouragement

Students may not be taught social skills in a classroom. Cooperative learning provides an appropriate setting for these skills to be taught.

293. Foster a commitment to the group through interdependence. Each group member is dependent on the other members. Students will need to work together.

294. Assess individual achievement by holding students accountable for their own learning by giving individual quizzes, tests, and written papers during a cooperative learning lesson.

295. Students need to review how they worked as a group. You can provide them a form or you can ask them for oral feedback. You should also provide them with feedback about what you observed during the lesson.

4.
Teaching the Lesson

296. Be ready to teach every day. Fumbling around for markers, transparencies, lunch count sheets, and other materials takes valuable learning time. Arrive fifteen to thirty minutes early just to arrange your materials and your lesson.

297. Do an "energizer" when you know that student energy is low. Energizers only need to be thirty seconds, and can be very effective at the beginning of the day, after lunch, or at the end of the day. Some examples include getting students on their feet, stretching, walking like monkeys for one minute, or doing the wave.

298. When students finish a project, test, or unit, celebrate. The celebration only needs to take a few minutes. You can have them give a thumbs up, give a high five, or stomp their feet. Students like to get involved in the celebration and express "a job well done."

299. Celebrate the learning curve that you will observe in your classroom from the beginning to the end of the year. Throw a popcorn party, send a good news note home, or let your students pick out a sticker.

300. Ensure that you have incorporated one question each day that is a thinking question instead of a fact-based question. A thinking question is open-ended and has more than one response. Plan one question to force students to ponder, combine ideas, or formulate new information. Put the question on the board, or type it in large font so you don't forget to ask the question.

301. Whenever you assign a big project or a research paper, break the project into manageable sections for the students. Some students will do this automatically; others need the direct instruction and step-by-step procedures to help them organize and manage such a major project. A few students will need a very detailed timeline.

302. Keep families involved in their child's learning. Design supplemental at-home activities that augment the concepts students are learning at school. Include clear and concise instructions and the reason why you are sending the materials home. Many parents do not know what their child is learning and why they need to learn certain concepts. Educate the parents as well.

303. Avoid interruptions during the school day. You can place a sign on the door or ask the administration, counselors, and other staff not to disturb your class during instructional times unless there is an emergency. Uninterrupted time in a classroom is premium learning time. When students are distracted, it takes time to refocus their attention.

304. Conduct research on curriculum before a curriculum workshop. Know what your school's data tells you about the students in your building. Bring your standards and benchmarks to the meeting. Call other districts to seek information about their curriculum. Be prepared.

305. Recognize that mediocrity is not an option for you or for your students. Meeting each of your students' unique needs requires intensity, purpose, creativity, and a strong focus on student achievement. Motivate your students to do their very best by involving students in their learning through a variety of opportunities.

306. Students will ask the inevitable: "Why do we have to learn this?" Be quick to answer by drawing connections to real life situations, jobs, and experiences.

307. Show students ways to search for information on their own. In the age of information, students need to know credible places to find the answers. Help them to navigate the school library and computer lab.

308. Show your students that learning is an ongoing process, even for adults. Ask students to interview adults from various backgrounds about how they have to continue to learn new skills. As a class, formulate the questions that will be asked. Assign students to computer generate the interview script. The learning and sharing of information will support the message that learning never stops.

309. Motivate your students to do their best by providing lessons that are relevant, rigorous, and that build relationships between and among concepts.

Presentation

310. Deliver important announcements from one spot in the room. Lower your voice. Wait until you have students' attention. Whenever you have something that students really need to listen to, stand in the same spot, wait, and talk to the students in a voice that is softer than normal. They will soon recognize that when you walk to that spot all eyes and ears need to be alert for essential information. For example, you will stand in that area when you announce changes in a project's requirements or an upcoming test or event.

311. As soon as possible in the school year, begin to display student work. Elementary schools are alive with work that shows what students are learning. Middle school and high school teachers should also display appropriate projects. Ask to use the media center or cafeteria to display larger projects.

312. Deliver instructions orally *and* written out in either a handout or on the board. Some students are primarily visual learners and other students are primarily auditory learners. You need to ensure that you're effectively reaching all students.

313. Clearly state instructions in a step-by-step or bulleted format. Students cannot begin a lesson or will start with wrong assumptions if the directions are not simple, concise, and clear. Take time to craft your lesson plan in an easy-to-follow format.

314. When instructing students, be animated, use gestures, voice inflection, and walk about to keep student interest and focus. Some teachers are naturals at this but others have difficulty developing these skills.

315. Appeal to your students' five senses to enhance the learning process. When students can divide a pie in eighths, they more readily understand the concept of division. When students experience hot and cold changes in a lab experiment, they are learning the rules of thermodynamics.

316. Videotape yourself teaching a lesson. This can be very painful, but you will also be able to see the annoying tics, "ums," and the lack of movement. Use this information to help your overall presentation in the classroom.

Incorporate Something Creative into Every Lesson

317. Design lessons that allow students to teach something. Set the model and give your students the freedom to design their own strategies to increase participation and learning. Teaching is one of the most effective ways to learn.

318. Use stories and anecdotes to connect learning with real life situations. Students will remember the story and then link it to the concept.

319. Use graphics to help students with organizing information from text. Many students need the visual image of organized thoughts to help them compile information.

320. Support students' sense of curiosity by providing opportunities to investigate, probe, and uncover information. Supply multiple ways students can accomplish their task and present it in various forms.

321. Begin reading aloud a passage of a novel or short story to students. You can do this at any grade level from elementary through high school. By reading aloud, you have engaged the student, and they are more likely to continue reading.

322. Form groups and have students write story problems for math concepts that they have been studying. Students use comprehension, creativity, and problem-solving skills to help them write the problems, plus problem-solving skills to help them solve the problem.

323. Do mental activities with your class when a few minutes are left during the class period or day. Such activities keep students' thinking sharp and activated. Use trivia questions, problem solving questions, or current event questions.

324. Construct learning centers that will exercise learning, promote inquiry, and provide challenges. When students have explored many of the learning options, design another learning center to optimize skills and concepts. Build on the concepts or skills that you are identifying in the lessons by designing the centers around the areas of math, science, and reading. You can also plan learning centers around the fine arts areas, themes, or specific topics such as engineering, cities, volcanoes, jewelry making, or Valentine celebration.

325. Do not underestimate the "show and tell" days of the early grades. Show and tell is the beginning of preparing students to speak before a group. Give students plenty of opportunities for public speaking. The more young students hear each other speak, the faster they will develop their own skills.

326. When you are teaching, use words that are descriptive and lively, provide several examples to support the concept, and try to teach a lesson relevant to the world of work. Students need to continue to see the relevance (Why do we have to learn this?) and they need to cement their learning in examples.

327. Offer real-life learning experiences for students by visiting local factories, business establishments, and governmental agencies. Try to provide hands-on experiences for the students whenever appropriate. Hold students accountable for their learning by asking them to give feedback that summarizes their experience.

328. Foster discovery, invention, inquiry and artistic creations through meaningful lessons that will promote synthesis and evaluation. Students need to be challenged to think beyond the usual conventions in the classroom.

329. Facilitate video viewing by keeping some lights on. If you shut off all the lights, the students will be tempted to fall asleep. Provide a strategy that students can use to take notes, highlight the important parts, or remember key terms. Always hold students accountable for paying attention by having a discussion, a quick whip of ideas where everyone participates, or a short writing exercise after the video.

330. Share some of your interests, collections, and prized treasures with your students. Bring your favorite CD, kindergarten picture, diplomas, and family pictures. Periodically change what you have displayed. You'll continue to build a closer relationship with your students, and the items will provide more things to talk about with your students.

Emphasize Key Learning Attributes at All Levels and Subjects

331. Supplement classes with a variety of reading material in your class or grade level. Students need to be reading a variety of materials including fiction, non-fiction, poetry, technical manuals, and newspapers. Learning occurs through many types of genre.

332. All teachers will become reading teachers to various degrees. The goal of reading instruction is to impart strategies, skills, and knowledge to foster five areas: phonemic awareness, phonics, fluency, comprehension, and vocabulary. Reading instruction does not stop at sixth grade, but needs to be taught throughout the system at all grade levels. As the complexity of material increases, research-based strategies need to be introduced or reviewed to help older readers with varying types of text.

333. Establish a reading environment in all classrooms. Bring books you are reading to class and talk about them. Students are curious about what their teachers do. Modeling reading sends a potent message to students.

334. Help students become aware of their thought process as readers. Explain how their thought process will help them become a better reader and a better learner. To learn how to do this, take a class, read about strategies that work in the classroom, or attend a workshop. Ask the district if it will pay for your registration to a workshop or conference.

335. Teach vocabulary daily. Keep the words posted on a wall connected with clues, books, or references that serve as reminders for students. Use drawings or pictures as definitions or clues to help students remember. Review or add more words each week. This is appropriate for all grade levels, from elementary students through high school.

336. You are the chief learner in the classroom. With the emphasis on teaching reading, math, and science skills, learn as much as you can to help your students become better readers, mathematicians, and scientists. Model strategies for students and have them practice the strategies until they automatically use them.

337. Use what you learn in staff development seminars in the classroom. Keep an implementation log which documents how many times you used the strategies you learned over a period of time. Not only will the strategies help your students, but you will also be able to produce the evidence that you used the strategies.

338. Find explicit, easy ways to involve families in a student's reading development. Give them specific ways they can help their child become proficient in reading. Children need to be reading at home as well as in school because it takes student, teacher, and parent to achieve academic success.

339. Develop a reading log to send home with students that records the time spent on reading at home and provides a space for comments from the parents. Students can read to grandparents, brothers and sisters, aunts and uncles, neighbors, and parents or guardians. The reading journal is returned on Monday to the teacher who comments and returns the journal to the families for continued use.

340. Bridge the gap between teachers in the same content area or the same grade level who aren't working together. Begin by initiating conversations about curriculum, instruction and assessment.

341. Discuss differences in paragraph structure with your students to help them understand the texts they're reading. Paragraph structures such as compare and contrast, sequencing, and chronological order are common in student texts.

342. Read to your students. Every teacher is a reading teacher. Reading is in every content area and a teacher is responsible for teaching vocabulary, comprehension, and fluency in all content areas. Select books that align with your curriculum and help provide additional education.

Testing and Grading

343. Organize students in pairs to review for a test or a quiz. Students learn from each other. Give them sample test questions to study. Encourage them to pair up outside of school by using the telephone, computer, or face-to-face meetings to continue to study and learn.

344. Assist students in organizing study teams. Students gain support and help from each other. Show students how to work within a study team and provide strategies that they can use when studying in a group. They can create visual images, linking relationships, and mnemonic devices that will help them remember the key points.

345. Before students turn in their papers to you, instruct them to look over their paper for errors in a last minute proofreading. Relate to the students that many times mistakes are missed and that by glancing at the paper, quiz, or test one more time, they may find an error.

346. Carefully monitor when students correct each others papers. Each student's grade should be confidential. Safeguard their privacy by using this technique sparingly. A better system is to have the students correct their own paper since the student has a vested interest in his or her own learning and will learn from their mistakes instead of their neighbors mistakes.

347. Trust students to grade their own daily work. Tell them the purpose for doing their work is to practice and learn the concepts for themselves, not for you. Watch carefully as students correct the papers. Although you may not count the scores, you don't want students to practice cheating.

348. Refrain from grading papers with a red ink pen. Use a green pen which is a more positive color and also signals to the reader to "GO" ahead and make revisions. When correcting, use a slash instead of a large "X," which is a more negative symbol. When recording points, give the positive points, not a negative number. Add comments to the points.

349. When correcting papers, give positive feedback and praise their improvement. Give suggestions for revisions when appropriate, and allow students to do their own correcting.

350. Watch for students who are cheating. While there are many reasons why they might cheat, they are robbing themselves and others of a fair chance to be assessed. Take the student aside, explain the consequences, and give the student time to explain his or her position. Think ahead of time about the consequences, such as awarding no credit for the test or paper.

351. Find a place that is away from students and colleagues to correct papers, prepare lessons, or organize your day. Make sure that it is quiet and has few interruptions so that you can concentrate during your prep period.

Understand Unique Learning Styles

352. Know your learning styles. How do you learn best? Then remember that not all learners learn that way. Be flexible by incorporating different activities to match the various learning styles.

353. Determine how your middle school and high school students learn best by asking them to respond to a survey, a few questions, or by observation. Your students will be able to state their preferred learning style. Consider this as you group students and instruct them. If you primarily teach to a student's weaker style, he or she will not learn as quickly or as easily.

354. Learning preferences generally include the following:

- Visual Learners—need visual representations such as maps, pictures, charts, graphs, and drawings; known to form mental pictures; become concrete learners, need visual stimuli
- Auditory Learners—need to hear information first to synthesize the facts; abstract thinkers who value harmonious sounds and conversation
- Tactile/Kinesthetic Learners—learn by getting involved or by physically doing; tend to be active as they interact to build a skill, concept, or program

355. Awareness of these different learning styles will help in planning, instructing, and assessing students as you accommodate their learning needs. Take some time to research about individual learning styles.

356. Include the following when designing learning centers so that you maximize the enrichment each student will experience at the centers:

- The purpose of the station
- Clear, step-by-step, laminated directions to follow
- Materials placed carefully in a binder, folder, or container
- A sign-out sheet that includes a place for the student's response to the activity

357. If you are planning several learning centers, carefully consider the following:

- Ask another teacher for ideas or to share by rotating learning centers between rooms.
- Ask for parent or community volunteers to help with finding materials, laminating, and organizing.
- Keep the centers compact unless classroom space allows a larger area.
- Designate times when students can use the learning centers.
- Keep data on who has used the centers and who has not had an opportunity.

358. Understand that your textbook is a tool. You need to use many tools in your classroom to supplement learning.

359. Although textbooks in recent years have become more appealing and engaging to students, be aware that many are either too difficult for students to read or are too jammed with text, graphs, pictures, text boxes, and other gimmicks to make a page look more attractive. If your textbook seems too difficult for your students, check the readability level. If it is too difficult for many of your readers, you may have to use other strategies to help students gain a better understanding of the material.

360. Use your textbook as a supplemental text and inculcate information through the use of outside sources and books. The curriculum becomes more fascinating, exciting, and more informative.

Assigning Homework

361. Determine what you want students to learn and be able to do from a homework assignment. Don't give repetitive assignments to everyone if a majority of the students already understand the concepts covered.

362. Contemplate providing differentiated assignments to serve your purpose. Differentiation means to change the type of lessons, the purpose, and the level of assignments. Provide projects, performances, and demonstrations that match student interests and their learning needs.

363. Establish a homework policy that is clear to both students and parents. Send the policy and expectations to parents/guardians and students, hand them the policy when they attend open house, post the policy in the room, and reiterate that policy until the students internalize it. In the policy, state the following:

- Reasons why you believe homework to be important
- How much to expect each night
- The standard for acceptance
- Expectations for completing homework when students are absent
- Consequences of late homework assignments

364. Find out how long your homework assignments are taking students to finish. Think about your students' schedules and lives when assigning homework. For elementary and middle school students, two hours is too much for one class. If every high school teacher gave two hours of homework, students taking four subjects could have eight hours of homework a night. Students would work from 5:00 p.m. until 1:00 a.m. Be reasonable in your expectations. Some assignments will take more time than other assignments, but be cognizant of that and tell students what work will take longer.

365. Collecting and grading homework can be overwhelming in specific content areas. In particular, if you have five sections or classes, you may feel buried by assignments. Don't procrastinate. Begin correcting work as soon as possible to avoid stress.

366. Establish a system to gather students' work. You may feel besieged with late assignments and student absenteeism. Ask students to put a sticky note on the assignment and the date that they submitted the work. Make this process as simple as possible for you and for the students.

367. Develop a system for posting homework assignments and the date they're due. You can put this on the board, on the website, on the assignment, and in the area where you keep the handouts and homework folders. A designated area keeps you and the students organized.

368. At the elementary level, send a calendar home to parents. Ask that they post the calendar of activities (homework) on the refrigerator and follow the directions every evening. Parents need to have a process and a set focus for helping with the homework. Be specific with directions.

Planning for a Substitute

369. If you need a substitute teacher remember to leave them the following information:

- Class roster and seating chart
- Classroom rules
- Directions for taking attendance, going to lunch, and allowing students to leave the classroom
- A detailed plan for the day's lesson
- The schedule for the day

It is your responsibility to structure a lesson that will keep students engaged. By doing this, you will also minimize classroom management problems for the substitute.

370. Ask the teacher to write you a follow-up note after subbing in your classroom. Divide the note into two categories with the positive comments on one side and the "needs improvement" comments from the substitute on the other side.

371. Prepare your students for a substitute teacher by reviewing the rules of the classroom. Tell students what you will expect of them when you are absent. When you return, provide feedback to the class about their behavior and academic accomplishments.

372. Think ahead and prepare a folder for emergency situations when you can't make it to school to plan a lesson. The folder will be available in a drawer for emergencies only. Prepare three days of such instructional materials for a substitute teacher.

373. Plan for special days, assemblies, disruptions due to weather, and other things that hinder the flow of learning. Keep a schedule for the next week on your desk as a quick reference. Provide this information to substitutes so that they can be prepared.

5.
Assessing Student Learning

374. Assessing, or testing, is to check for understanding of what the students know. When we find out what the student does not know, we teach new concepts by using the most effective strategies to help the student learn.

375. Before you start the school year, understand the grading system and report card that is distributed to the students from your school system. Mark the timelines on your calendar when grades are due. A grading system is just one way for a school to document student achievement.

376. Remember that one of the purposes of assessment is to help the teacher make good decisions on appropriate instruction. When analyzing assessment data, think about what resources and strategies will help your students improve academically.

377. It is the best practice to collaborate with a team to determine what approach of instruction will help an underachieving student achieve. The collaboration model will also work when designing behavior plans for students.

378. Let the student know what they are going to learn when teaching a lesson. Write the purpose of the lesson on the board for the student to see visually as well. Assess what you have taught them.

379. Teach students test-taking strategies. We teach students the how-tos in every subject, but rarely do we take time to show students how to take or study for a test. Students will score better on a test when they have test-taking tips to follow.

380. Students should know the importance of arriving on time the day of an exam so they have the full time period to complete the test. Teach them the importance of pacing themselves so they do not spend too much time on one particular area of the test.

381. Walk around the room when students are taking tests. It is too easy to begin working on uncorrected papers or preparing for the next activity. When students are working, this is prime time to observe and assist students with questions.

Top 5 Test-Taking Strategies That Work

382. Tell students to read all the way through the test before they begin, and answer all of the questions they are sure of first before going back and completing the test.

383. Tell students to pay attention to questions that have more point values and that will have the most influence on their final test grade.

384. Teach students how to answer essay questions. Explain to them how to make a brief outline with key points before they begin to write their answer.

385. Tell students to proofread their test before submitting it to the teacher to be scored if time permits. Taking a deep breath and relaxing for a moment will help the students to re-examine their work for errors or additions to be made.

386. Remind students to always write their first and last names on their tests. It would be unfortunate if you could not give students credit because there is no name on the work.

Test Reading and Writing on a Regular Basis

387. Oral book reports can be a form of assessment; however, they must have criteria for the students to follow. Students should be expected to read the book and be able to discuss the author, the content, and why they enjoyed the book.

388. Writing assignments can vary from expressing ideas, to writing the facts, or both. Be clear what the writing assignment will be about and what will actually be graded.

389. Post in your classroom common mechanical rules that you expect students to know such as format, spelling, font, and grammar.

390. The ultimate goal in teaching writing is that students can improve their written expression. This will take practice and coaching from you. Always provide feedback.

391. The more a student writes, the better at writing he or she will be. Encourage your students to write for the school newspaper, or write letters to family and friends. Offer essay questions for bonus points on the next exam.

392. It is important to give students clear directions in a writing assignment and let them know what will be graded. The extent to which you grade on content and mechanics should be stated when you give the assignment.

393. Teach your students the what, when, why, and where to explain an event. This strategy helps students clearly express themselves in writing.

Preparing Your Students for Standardized Tests

394. Emphasize the importance of standardized tests. Make sure your students know why they are important and why they have to take them. Whether or not you agree or disagree with high-stakes testing, you must act appropriately and professionally. If you do not buy in to the standardized testing, students will follow your lead and react the same way. This can translate into lower test scores.

395. Review the data from standardized tests with the students. Students are the last to know about what the testing results indicate. Use this teachable moment to make graphs of their scores, write letters to parents/guardians about the results, or utilize computer software to organize the information.

396. Keep a folder on each student with the results of the standardized testing. This can be paper-based or in a computer program. This will provide a snapshot view of student progress and will help you to formulate a course of study.

397. Prepare your students for standardized tests throughout the school year. Because so much emphasis is placed on standardized tests results, working with your students throughout the year is worthwhile.

398. It is your responsibility to closely monitor students when they are taking standardized tests. Walk around the room and make sure they are not just filling in the dots or making a design.

399. Math standardized tests will probably not allow students to use calculators. Have students make flash cards and review the basics with a partner until they have the facts memorized. Older students may think this is a waste of time, but the review will help them remember what they often forget with continual calculator use.

400. When working on complex math problems, teach students to narrow down the choices when they are not sure of an answer on a standardized test. Explain how to make the best educated guess in these situations.

401. Many assessments, especially standardized tests, have true/false and multiple-choice questions. Teach students to read the questions carefully and cross out the answers they know are incorrect if they reach the point of having to guess the answer.

402. When teaching students to take standardized tests, train them to ask themselves specifically what each individual question is asking. For example, the English test may consist of reading passages, but instead of comprehension, it may be asking for correct or incorrect grammar or spelling.

403. Standardized tests often have a time limit. Write the time on the board when the test will be over to help students pace their time.

404. If allowed, give students a five-minute warning before a test is to end. If you do not hear about whether or not this is allowed in the orientation, ask the administration.

405. Tell students to answer the questions they know first and then go back and answer the questions they did not know. Mark the questions they skipped with a slight pencil mark so they remember to go back.

406. Remind students to make sure their question and answer number on the grid sheet are the same. It is easy to get off when not answering the questions in order.

407. Students can prepare for standardized tests by memorizing some basic rules in skill areas such as spelling and math.

408. Have students make flash cards with spelling and grammar rules. Even though there are exceptions to the rules, the review will help them with many of the questions.

409. Remind students when reading passages not to read more into the passage than is written and also not to debate what is being read. Read the passages with the specific questions on the test in mind.

410. Ask students to bring in #2 pencils the day before the test and have them sharpened. This ensures that the class is not busy using the pencil sharpener just before taking the standardized test. Keep #2 pencils sharpened and available for when students' pencils break.

411. Many schools will keep the actual standardized test under lock and key, and they will not be distributed until the day of the test. The teacher testing manuals might be with the test so if the administrator does not give you a copy of the manual, request that you have the opportunity to read the instruction manual ahead of time.

412. All staff should be trained in standardized testing procedures to support consistency in standardized testing administration and participation of the students. If you do not receive training, ask colleagues about testing procedures and the scheduling of classes during testing periods.

413. Scheduling for standardized tests will be school wide. The entire building will be on the same schedule for the sake of consistency.

414. Ask the administration what the policy is for standardized makeup tests. Even though the school will stress that every student be in school for standardized testing, there will be exceptions and, as the teacher, you need to be aware of what to do for your students who missed the test. There is usually a time frame for tests to be returned to the company for scoring.

415. The stakes are high for standardized testing, but do not bribe your students with rewards such as a day off from school or other unreasonable incentives just to get them to perform well.

416. Tests results for individual students are private, but group reports and school reports are public record. Schools must report their standardized test results to the public via the school newsletter, a public meeting, or the local newspaper.

417. After you score a test, take the time to schedule appointments with students to review their essay tests and address any problems or concerns they may have with understanding the subject matter.

418. When designing essay tests, be sure to teach students how to write logical answers. If you do not teach students how to write a clear answer, most students will not have the skills to organize their thinking. Tell students to read their answers to themselves to make sure they make sense before handing them in.

419. Use test results to springboard ideas for improvement. Explore opportunities to expand in other areas. Offer independent learning projects for students who need additional practice in specific areas.

420. Find out what students know about a subject before you begin a unit. You can find out what students know by observation, asking questions, or surveying the class with a five point quiz. Use the data to help design the unit.

421. Occasionally allow students to evaluate their own work. Self-evaluations assist students in assessing their learning and provide the teacher with multidimensional assessment information about the student for the final grade.

422. If a student did not receive a passing grade on a test, find a way to remediate immediately. Students need immediate feedback especially if they are failing. He or she may need one-on-one instruction, as well as a plan to get back on the right path of success. You may have to reconstruct the individual student learning.

423. Have students highlight and summarize key points they have learned at the end of your class or the end of the day. Write the comments on the board for everyone to see, and remind them they can tell their families when they go home at night that this is what they learned in school today.

424. Review your school handbook about student grievances concerning grades. Establish with your class the process if a student should disagree with the grade they have received. If you should become involved in a grade dispute, document your meetings, the date, and issues of concern.

425. Teach students how to read their assessment results. Next, show students how to make graphs of their scores. This will help students learn on two levels—personal and instructional.

426. Analyze assessment data that will show students where they are and where they should be. Keep a healthy dialogue about why they are learning the curriculum and the processes that are being assessed. The day-to-day forms of assessment are to encourage improvement as well as affirm what students have already mastered.

427. Provide various opportunities for students to collect data. Teach them how to gather, analyze, and present their findings. Action research is a powerful way to empower students to draw conclusions about their own learning processes based on their own research.

428. Require students to keep their grades from daily work projects, tests, and quizzes in a notebook or on the computer so they will know in a glance their grade. Students should learn to keep track of their own academic performance and progress.

429. Solicit student feedback by asking them how they view themselves as learners and as test takers. Encourage them to give you honest answers so you can work together to improve their learning techniques.

430. Let students choose the work they want to display for performance assessment, such as writing, art, or woodworking. Change the displayed work often so everyone has an equal opportunity to be spotlighted.

431. Give the students opportunities to submit drafts for revisions. If they understand your recommendations are for revisions, they will welcome your comments and realize that revising is part of the writing process.

432. Offer opportunities for students to share their performance talents in the classroom. This will give students who are talented in areas other than academics the opportunity to showcase their talents.

433. Review with your class before a test by devising a review game, developing skits, or creating other activities that help students remember concepts. By reviewing as a class, everyone is involved in teaching and learning from each other.

434. Allow your students to have opportunities to present their data to fellow students, school faculty, the city council, or citizens groups. This experience provides students with multiple learning opportunities, such as public speaking, that will be beneficial to them in future years.

Documenting Progress and Grading

435. Carefully document student progress, and be able to support the findings. Administrators, parents/guardians, and students want to know where the student stands academically and the reasons the student has improved or digressed.

436. A student's potential is measured by more than just grades. Consider how well he or she participates, shows initiative, processes information, and is engaged in learning. Your observation skills and conversations with the student will assist you with understanding the potential of the student. Make this even more concrete by developing rubrics, checklists, or note cards to record student progress.

437. Compile daily and weekly assessments as a way to measure, in small increments, whether or not the students are meeting the required objectives. This will help you troubleshoot problems early, and you can help the students immediately instead of waiting for poor test results.

438. Track student data on graphs to visually show progress. Graphs will show you trend lines in individual student and classroom performance. The information will assist with decision making for instruction and needs of your classroom.

439. Monitor student's progress by keeping track of daily work, class participation, and assessments. Give recognition to students that turn in their daily assignments by writing their names on the board instead of making the list of who has not turned in their work.

440. There are software programs that can assist you with records to keep track of grades. Many schools will have district-wide systems that you will need to learn before the school year begins. Record keeping is usually part of your new teacher orientation.

441. Schools must keep student records for a period of several years. Their permanent records should be kept in a fireproof safe or file cabinet. If you take the folders out of the office you will most likely have to sign them in and out. It is best to read the cumulative folders, which is a culmination of student information in the office workroom if possible. It is not recommended you leave the building with the permanent records.

442. Provide parents/guardians time to ask questions about assessments, testing material, and results. Avoid using educational terms and jargon. Instead, use visual representations like graphs and charts.

443. Schools use report cards to report student progress to parents. As a teacher you will be responsible for filling out a report card for each student. Review the report card before the school year begins so you know what type of documentation you will be using to report progress to the parents/guardians.

444. Always keep a paper or electronic copy of the report card that you sent to the parents. The copy will serve as a back up in case anything happens to the report card sent home.

445. Some school systems have honor rolls. At your new teacher orientation ask about the criteria for making the honor roll.

446. You will be responsible for submitting the names for the honor roll to the central office for publication. Make sure you have calculated the grade points accurately.

447. Before distributing the report cards to the parents take the time to conference with each student about his or her past nine weeks of work. Students are responsible for their own grades and need to be able to be articulate to their parents about their grades.

448. Do not publicly post test scores with student names or with a code that is easy to identify the student. The posting code name is between you and the student and is not for public knowledge.

449. Continual observation of your students outside of the classroom will assist you with an assessment of how they are doing in school. Observe how they perform in their extra-curricular activities as well as their social interactions.

6.
Utilizing Resources

450. At the beginning of the school year, ask parents to partner with you as the guide and facilitator of their child's education. Provide a preview of the year and concepts that students will need to learn. Ask them to be involved partners in the process. Some parents truly believe it is the school's job and do not feel comfortable being involved. Other parents will not want to participate because of time or personal issues. Respect their wishes, but let them know you will still keep them informed.

451. Study the history and style of composers and musical groups, so that students have a deeper understanding than just liking or disliking the music.

452. Have students lead book talks in small groups (literature circles). Book talks are opportunities for students to tell about the books they are reading. They will learn summarization as well as presentation skills doing book talks.

453. Make sure every student has a dictionary and is comfortable using it as a resource. If not everyone can afford to buy a dictionary, you can ask for donations for your classroom.

454. Stress to the families that there is not a need for the most expensive supplies—the basic supplies will accomplish most tasks.

455. Every student should have access to three libraries.

- School libraries contain books related to academics and books that support what is being taught in the classrooms.
- Public libraries expand upon the school library and are diverse enough to meet everyone's needs.
- Personal libraries should consist of what students really love to read! This library is each student's personal choice.

456. Support and remind students and their families of their three libraries, and include this as part of a homework assignment. An example would be that they visit the public library as a family one time a semester and receive extra credit in your class for doing this activity. Since this is an after school assignment that is dependent on support from others, ask students to visit with you if there is an issue about going to the library.

457. Take a field trip to the public library, and make sure every student has a library card. Invite their families or neighbors to go on this field trip with you. If possible, visit the library with your class at least once a semester.

458. Teach students to be good stewards of books. Remind them that the books in the school and public library are on loan to them and will be shared with many others. They need to be treated carefully. Keep library books in a special place, and travel with them in a bag.

459. Join the public library club, and encourage others to do the same. For example, the library club might be called "Friends of the Library," and do volunteer work to keep the library a great place to visit for everyone.

460. Get in the habit of reading the newspaper in the library. This will save you from purchasing the newspaper and will take you to the library every day.

461. Check out magazines from the library to save on subscriptions. If you want a particular article for further reference, make a copy.

462. Invite friends to join you at the library. Some libraries have coffee shops with the proceeds used to support the library. If you're new to an area, these coffee shops can be a great place to meet people.

463. Introduce yourself to the librarian. He or she will be a great resource for you and may be more inclined to work with you and your students personally if she knows you. Partner with the librarian in setting up after school book clubs for students.

464. Help students build their home libraries through book exchanges, used book sales, garage sales, or by requesting books as Christmas gifts. Many students are unable to purchase books.

465. Ask the librarian to offer help sessions when students are working on research. Librarians will instruct students on the best way to search for material, both on the Internet and throughout the library.

466. In collaboration with the librarian, design a "Meet the Authors Day" when students can listen to authors talk about the process of writing and publishing. Students find this very informative when it ties into their reading and writing.

467. When selecting books for students to read in class, study the authors and their history and writing style. This information will help the student develop a taste for reading and book selection.

468. Build a library of books in your classroom. Ask for hanging shelves, sleeves, or bookcases. If you don't have the resources, use bricks and boards. Every classroom should be full of books that students can use as resources.

469. Check out a piece of art from the library or a museum for the classroom. Incorporate the artwork in a lesson that you are teaching.

470. Check out books to use in your classroom. Some public libraries are allotted funding based on their usage, so they will be happy to work with you in the book selection process to align with your curriculum.

Book Fairs and Used Book Sales

471. Book companies will be glad to set up book fairs as fundraisers for your school to purchase more books. Fundraising book fairs are usually set up by your parent club and are often combined with another school activity like parent-teacher conferences.

472. Parent groups will welcome recommendations from teachers concerning hosting a book fair. If a book company asks for suggestions, recommend that they offer books that align with the district curriculum goals. If there are bookstores in your community, recommend they be asked about hosting a book fair.

473. Request that book fair companies sell books, and not trinkets. The purpose of a book fair is to make students and families aware of the best sellers, reader's choice books, and the most current books in circulation.

474. Have used book sales or exchanges. Keep prices affordable for all students. Reading and conversation about books is the goal.

475. Participate in a used book sale as a class. This is a great way to keep books in circulation. The money raised can be used to purchase more books for the library.

Partnerships

476. Collaborate with others to enrich instruction. Your colleagues are valuable resources. Utilize their knowledge and experience by building relationships, asking questions, and seeking advice.

477. Some students are uncomfortable with cooperative and collaborative learning. Try to recognize this trait in your more introverted students, and make adjustments.

478. Think of ways to link struggling students with outside partners to help them through the bumps. Clear this with the building principal before you begin the process. Volunteers must apply in the school office and have a clearance check.

479. Training for volunteers has to be provided by either the volunteer coordinator or the administration. The volunteer program should be based on input from the staff. As a teacher, think of the best way to utilize volunteers to improve student achievement.

480. Partner with your district grant writer and search for grants that extend learning opportunities for you and for your students. If your district does not have a grant writer, visit with your administration about the possibility of hiring a person to write grants.

Job Shadow and Career Days

481. Students should participate in job shadow and career days with people in the community and with their parents or guardians. Help students see that learning is lifelong. Students will have a better idea of what adults do during their workday.

482. In preparation for a job shadow day, have students research various careers that are of interest to them. Have them select their top three choices and then contact the person that would be the shadow host. The first choice may not be possible, so it is best to have other options.

483. Discuss with the job site and your students appropriate attire for the day. Participants will be expected to dress appropriately for their job experience. Remind students that they are representing your school.

484. Either the school or the student will have to arrange transportation on a job shadow day. You must verify in writing how students are reaching their destination. Travel information should be on the permission slip signed by the parents/guardians.

485. The students and the workplace should have a one-page evaluation sheet to complete about the experience. The evaluation sheet should include questions for the students about the experiences they had and what they learned, and recommendations from the host on how to improve the process in the future. Students will be expected to write thank-you notes to the job site contact following the experience.

Community Resources

486. Help your students organize a food drive some time other than Christmas. Call the local food pantry and ask when they could use your help the most throughout the year.

487. Plan field trips to industries and businesses that require a particular background. Ask the employees to describe what they do and to make explicit the requirements for the occupations.

488. Visit a bank so students can see the relevance of understanding numbers and the importance of accuracy and detail. Ask an employee to talk specifically to the students at a level that they can comprehend.

489. Locate the local senior citizen center and set up an appointment to meet with their board about the possibilities of utilizing their resources and time. They can make bulletin boards, cut out letters, tutor students, or speak to classes.

490. When planning units in science, math, reading, or other subject areas, brainstorm any ways that community groups can support the unit with presentations, displays, hands-on experiments, and materials.

491. Ask the lumber store if they can cut you handheld white boards for your students to use instead of chalkboards. Chalkboards are dusty for students with allergies, and the white boards can come in handy for assessment and classroom instruction.

492. Ask parents and community volunteers to help during special days. They are usually very willing to assist. Give them their assignment with directions before they come. You will avoid confusion or taking time to explain what you want them to do. If parents choose not to assist, ask them if they have a friend or someone else that can assist.

493. Partner with local universities and colleges. They have many folks who are willing to talk with students about their areas of expertise. If a college or university is the host site for a student event, ask if the admissions counselor can give the students a brief tour of the campus and materials about the programs they offer.

494. Ask the local senior citizen's center to sew book bags to be checked out in the library or in your room. These bags could contain a book and supplemental activities for elementary students to check out and take home. Used book bags or material should be on your wish list to help supply this project.

495. There are many places throughout the community to look or ask for free things for your school and classroom. Some of the following sources are:

- Newspaper and printing offices—useable scrap paper
- Lumber yard or contractors building sites—scrap lumber to use for blocks or building projects.
- Paint and wallpaper stores—sample wallpaper books to use for textbook covers
- Carpet stores—carpet samples to carpet your room or carpet pieces to use as magic carpets in your classroom
- Any store that has displays. Let the store know you could use the display for a particular project.

496. When asking for freebies, either you or your school custodian will be expected to pick up and provide a thank-you note with a donation receipt on your school letterhead to the donor.

497. Search for places where you can find costumes, furniture, or toys for very little money in your communities. Goodwill stores, Salvation Army stores, and garage sales are places for great finds.

498. Look around the school district to find personnel who would be willing to work with your students on special projects. Volunteers can always be utilized in the classroom and on field trips.

499. Ask food service if your class can help plan the menu for the school meals for the week. If they are a tax-funded food service it will create an understanding of school systems and will build relationships with others in the system. It would be an opportunity to infuse other curriculums like health, business, and math.

500. Have your students volunteer to read to other adults or children in the building. Practicing reading aloud builds fluency and confidence.

501. Build a web page where students can find their assignments posted and download the assignments and any supplemental material from home.

502. Ask people who work in technologically advanced jobs to talk with your students about the effect of technology on their work.

503. If a computer and printer are available in the classroom, keep the class web page available so that students can download information and documents from the classroom. Let technology work for you in an expedient way.

504. Provide students with websites that will supplement their learning. This is one way to extend learning that also reaches tactile and kinetic learning styles. Have students share websites with the class that they thought were useful. You or other trusted adults should check out the websites beforehand to be sure they are appropriate. Follow a criterion that aligns with your school's standards and benchmarks for using the Internet during class time at school.

505. Be adept at navigating the Internet. The world is at your fingertips. Internet resources can be overwhelming, and you might want to divide and conquer the task by assigning students or volunteers to research particular areas.

506. Students love to take pictures, be in pictures, and look at pictures. Let students use the school camera and tell stories in pictures. Be sure to train them in the proper care and use of someone else's property.

507. Explore the many computer programs available for language development. Students benefit from a multimedia approach.

508. Utilize email for correspondence with government officials in your social studies classes so that students learn how they can affect their own government instantly.

509. Review with your students Internet usage and email policies of your school district. The student and parent should sign off on a school form that they are aware of the policies and procedures. You need to keep this information on file should there be an issue.

510. Use United streaming (www.united streaming.com) in the classroom to load videos for future viewing. You can order a video to be viewed at any time because it is downloaded onto the computer.

511. Post classroom guidelines and school policy for Internet use in a visible area of the classroom. Remind students every time they are in the computer lab.

512. Search for teacher friendly websites or sites that are content oriented. You will gain a plethora of information to be used in the classroom. Check with your state education department for content area websites, especially in math and science.

513. Become part of an online teacher discussion group. When you attend state and national conferences, you will be asked for your email address and to be put on a list for discussion groups. These groups can be an excellent source of information and a follow-up from the conferences.

514. Call a technology representative and ask about the latest software products in your content area. Always request a thirty-day trial, because the software may not be what you need to enhance your curriculum.

515. Use a Proxima digital projector in the classroom. Your media center should have one that you can check out to use in your classroom. Projecting the information on the big screen is another way to present information as students work with the material.

516. Instruct students in utilizing Power-Point for their presentations. As soon as the teacher thinks the students are ready they should create a PowerPoint presentation. Many students are capable of this skill in 4th grade.

517. With special needs students, find out the latest in assistive technology. With technological breakthroughs happening every day, the latest invention may be the tool that will help students accelerate their learning.

518. Find educational conferences where they hand out free samples and supplies. Posters, pens, and sample books will enhance your room and student learning. Conferences will be listed in professional development flyers, as well as education-oriented websites.

7.

Working with ESL Students

519. There has been a rapid growth of students enrolling in schools that do not speak English as their first language. Teachers need the awareness of the student's cultural background as well as the language proficiency level of their students.

520. Teaching students that do not speak English is challenging because of the language barrier, but it is by no means impossible. Speaking a different language does not qualify ESL students for special education classes. However, many of the strategies used in a special education classroom may work well with ESL students. Step-by-step instruction should be provided in direct, explicit language and then verbally explained.

521. Speech therapists are trained in language development and although students that speak another language do not necessarily need speech classes, speech therapists will be able to explain to you the language acquisition developmental process of children. Testing needs to be done in their first language to determine if the student would have a speech disorder.

522. Check with your administration or school assessment person to find out what assessment is used with students learning English for oral proficiency and placement in the academic areas. This will vary from state to state, but all English language learners must be assessed.

523. All English language learners are required to participate in the same rigorous curriculum that all students participate in as well as any district assessments. The guidelines may vary somewhat from state to state. Ask your administration to check with your state department of education for clarity of the assessment issues.

524. Ask the school to purchase novels in the student's native language to read when the class is reading a class novel. Students need to have literacy in their first language. Providing novels in their first language will enable students to keep up with the classroom discussions and activities that go with the novel.

525. Attendance is important for all of your students. Make sure that your non-English speaking students understand the attendance policies. If a student is not in class request a home visit to see if he or she is okay. As with any home visit, more than one person should go.

526. Become knowledgeable about the following terms used to describe the non-English speaking population you will be serving in your school. The terms are based on definitions used at federal and most state levels.

527. NEP—stands for the Non-English Proficient student.

528. LEP: Limited English Proficient—refers to a student who has a language background other than English, and proficiency in English is such that the probability of the student's academic success in an English-only classroom is below that of an academically successful peer with an English language background.

529. ELL: English Language Learner—refers to a national origin student who is limited-English proficient. This term is often preferred over LEP as it highlights accomplishments rather than limitations.

530. ESL: English as a Second Language—refers to a structured language acquisition program designed to teach English to students whose native language is other than English, until the student demonstrates a functional ability to speak, read, write, and listen to the English language at the age and agreed appropriate level.

531. BICS: Basic Interpersonal Communication Skills—language to carry on basic conversation—informal conversation, simple statements, and social exchanges.

532. CALP: Cognitive Academic Language Proficiency—language to learn academic information—writing, questioning, formal assessments.

533. The Language Proficiency Level of the student is the skill level in either the student's first language or their second language.

534. A translator that is skilled in the language can translate documents and forms for the school district. This is time-consuming so if you want notes sent home to be translated, allow enough turn-around time.

535. The second language the student is learning is referred to as L2. If the student's native language is German, and they are learning English, English would be their L2.

536. L1 is the native, primary, or the first language that a student speaks. Do not disregard the linguistic experiences and learning a student has from the time he or she is born until he or she comes to your school. Honor their first language as much as you can, as this is a part of who they are. It is appropriate for students to speak in the first language to their friends in the hall and at lunch. However, be sure to encourage the use of the language they are learning in the classroom.

537. A bilingual program model uses the student's first language, in addition to English, for instruction. The purpose of bilingual programs is to provide ELL students access to the school curriculum through use of the native language. If you are interested in bilingual programs visit the NABE (National Association of Bilingual Education) at www.nabe.org to learn more about successful bilingual programs.

538. Build on the background knowledge and prior experience of the ESL student and monitor their progress. Check for understanding as they progress in school. Do not assume someone comprehends the lesson just because his or her social English skills are improving.

539. Modifications to assignments and assessments are necessary for ESL students. Examples of types of modifications include the following:

- Allowing extra time
- Introducing vocabulary before each lesson
- Writing key words on the board
- Grading only what the student has completed
- Making a summary of the text for the student
- Showing verbs with body language
- Providing a bilingual dictionary that will include the English and the native language as well as a picture of the word

As you can imagine, many of the suggestions for modifications are good teaching and they will benefit many of your students that may be struggling to learn.

540. Language learning requires repetition. Music and nursery rhymes that have repetition are useful. Check out Mother Goose books, poetry books, rhyming books, and famous quotes. Visit the elementary classrooms in your district. They may have resources that you can borrow. Music, short songs, or jingles will also help your students remember words.

541. Use visuals, pictures, or artifacts to support the use of English. Using the props will help the students make connections to what they already know and what they are learning in English.

542. Use repetition of the same phrases and words to help with language development. As students learn words, put them in context, and check for understanding of usage.

543. Take the students on field trips to build vocabulary with the experiences. Use word walls, journals, and flip cards to review the vocabulary they learned.

544. Have students write their vocabulary words and sentences on white boards, overheads, and journals.

545. Do not worry about correct pronunciation at the beginning. It is most important that students are not self-conscious. Constant correction may hurt their self-confidence and discourage them from speaking.

546. Teach the new student basic survival words so he or she can be socially accepted by their peers. In addition to basic greetings, examples would include going through the lunch line and eating in the cafeteria, or going to the school library and checking out a book.

547. When the ESL students feel comfortable, have them share from their own experiences. The rest of your students will benefit from the ELS students' ethnic backgrounds. Assign all students to research their own heritage and share with the class.

548. If you are lecturing in class, make an audio tape and an outline of your lecture. ESL students can read (visual) and listen (auditory) to the information again at another time.

549. When teaching English Language Learners, think of your normal day routine and every task you take for granted. Your non-English speaking students will not have established a routine, nor will they know how to say the words in English that match what they see and do. Bring everyday routine items to your classroom to help them establish the conversation that goes with that routine.

550. Teachers need to know what the level is of student's oral English proficiency so that they have a baseline to begin teaching the student English. If the student arrives with no English speaking skills it seems obvious, but you will still have to collect assessment data. Time will need to be allowed for direct one-on-one English instruction or small group instruction outside of the classroom.

551. Partner reading, jigsaw reading (arranging pieces of a story in the correct order), and echo reading (having an ESL student repeat the words being read to them) are activities that help English Language Learners so they are not overwhelmed with all of the textbook reading that they will need to do in their classes.

552. Highlight textbooks to identify important vocabulary words and facts students need to know. Before they begin reading, write down the information you want them to find in the context and present the questions to them. As soon as they have read the passage ask the ELL or ESL students if they can answer the questions you asked them to look for in the reading.

553. Set language goals with your ESL students so they can track their accomplishments. Goals might include learning to say and write your name and their name, an understanding of U.S. currency, or the ability to speak and write where they came from and where they live today.

554. Use alphabet charts from the students' first languages and English side by side. Talk about the letters and the sounds that are the same and different. Use alphabet books in both languages.

555. Allow students to read books at their own pace, and give them support when needed. Select books that interest the students.

556. Begin the writing process by having ESL students tell you a story while you print the words on the paper. As students learn more words, have them begin to write their own stories.

Learn the Basics to Communicate

557. Learn a few words in the primary language of your student. Learn to say "hello," "welcome," and "glad you are in my class." You will be amazed how that will help begin to build the relationship between you, the student, and his or her family.

558. Learn the student's name and say it often to practice the pronunciation. Write the pronunciation on the board for everyone to visually see and practice. Help the student with your name by having him or her greet you and by writing your name on a card for him or her to see.

559. If your student's parents/guardians do not speak English, let the administration or office know that you will need an interpreter for conferences. Your request should be made a few weeks in advance, because there is often a shortage of interpreters and many schools will schedule conferences at approximately the same time of the year.

560. When using an interpreter for conferences or school meetings, try to keep messages to the point. Do not use professional jargon that the interpreter may not be able to translate. It will not only be difficult for the parent or guardian to understand, but you're risking the possibility that the jargon doesn't translate.

561. Communicate with the interpreter before and after the meeting to clarify the messages being delivered. Most likely, the school will have to hire the interpreter and you'll want to be assured it has been worth the time and expense for all involved.

562. Honor the first language of your student. If you ignore their first language and only concentrate on teaching the student English, you are not crediting the student for the learning process he or she has been engaged in since birth. Just as you would with any student, begin teaching from his or her strengths.

563. Use hand gestures, role-playing, and charades when teaching new concepts. Start with small groups so students do not feel self-conscious.

564. Print neatly on the board or overhead for your English Language Learner.

565. You do not need to talk louder when speaking to a non-English speaking student, but you do need to speak in a slow, clear voice.

566. Use words that they will hear often. Have one of your English speaking students make a list of words that you use often. If you feel uncomfortable having one of your students doing that task, tape your classroom instruction for a couple of hours and then listen for common words you use in instruction. This will be interesting for you as well as your students.

Make Your Classroom ESL Friendly

567. Be constructive with the time students have in your class. Collect catalogs and magazines to cut up and create picture dictionaries. Have books on tape to listen to, as well as materials for English Language Learners.

568. English speakers can create an English-to-second-language dictionary as well. This would be a good language partner activity.

569. Work with the media center in your school and request to have them purchase bilingual books with English/another language side-by-side with pictures. This will help ESL students with their language and help other students learn another language.

570. Schedule oral conversations with people who speak another language. One of the best ways for a child to learn another language is to practice with others in an informal conversation.

571. Investigate the possibility of exposing your students to a language lab. Students can listen to other languages on CDs or tapes every day for a short period of time. They must follow up with a verbal conversation to sustain what they have learned.

572. Language journals for your students—both the English speaking and English Language Learners—can help with their vocabulary skills.

573. Display a map in your classroom and mark the countries where your students come from. Use stickpins or colored dots to mark the countries. It will not be uncommon for you to have a diverse class.

574. Display money from other countries and show the comparison to U.S. currency. All students have a need to understand money, and they will be highly motivated to learn about the exchange of money.

575. As the person in charge of your classroom, model behaviors that value diversity and create an environment that is accepting and inclusive. Be friendly, fair, and kind to everyone.

576. Check out books about other cultures, and have them available in your classroom for the students to review. You can request your local library to borrow books for you from other libraries around the country if you cannot find the books you want.

577. Assign "language partners" to be mentors for the first month to assist with being a newcomer to the school. Expand the language partners to be family language partners and help them in the community. Schools cannot do this alone. When you ask for volunteers to be family language partners, this will help everyone have a better understanding of each other's culture. The new students will also be more likely to attend school functions if they have someone to go with.

578. To be a language partner, students must be fluent in English. They must be willing and patient to help the ESL student learn the language at a conversational level.

579. When grouping students, group the non-English speaking students with good, helpful students that will be welcoming and interested in them as individuals.

580. Provide times for students to interact with each other and discuss the lessons.

581. Invite your students to participate in a food fair, and make dishes of various cultures. However, do not ask your students to make food more than once a year. It is an expense and is problematic for some households, so be sensitive to the request for providing food.

Make an Effort to Educate Yourself

582. Many classroom teachers have not had training or experience in second language acquisition. Look for opportunities to become knowledgeable in this area.

583. Refer back to your alma mater for any programs inviting graduates to travel abroad or participate in language immersion experiences in the summer. You may be able to be a teacher's assistant if you have your Master's degree, or you may obtain graduate credit if needed.

584. Visit with the foreign language department chair in your school, and have his or her students visit your classroom and speak the language they are learning. If your school does not have a foreign language teacher, contact the closest university or public librarian.

585. Find out if your school offers trips for students to visit another country, and ask if you can be involved. You would most likely have to pay your own way, but sometimes chaperones receive a discount.

586. If you participate in the school trip, attend the planning meetings, meet the other participants, and learn the goals of the trip. Remember you are in an adult supervisory role.

587. Join language organizations such as TESOL (Teachers of English to Speakers of Other Languages, Inc.) or NABE (National Association for Bilingual Education). Both of these organizations provide a free journal with their membership fee as well as opportunities to learn and travel. They also have national conferences that are excellent sources of networking.

588. Contact your state department of education for possible teacher exchange programs in other countries. Exchange programs are offered for a semester or two to three weeks for graduate hours. If you have never experienced traveling out of the country, you may want to utilize this opportunity.

589. Inquire through the churches in the community of any missionary trips they might be planning. Missionary type trips usually last a few weeks. You are responsible for your own expenses, but a sister church or community may provide your lodging. Your purpose may possibly be to build a church or school. As a volunteer, you would work side-by-side with the people, which would be a great opportunity to become aware of the day-to-day living of another country.

590. Consider enrolling in an English Language endorsement program through a college or university. This will give you concrete knowledge in the best practice and research you need to meet the needs of the English Language Learners in your classroom. If you happen to work in an area short of teachers, you may qualify to participate in forgivable loan programs. Check with your department of education if your location is considered a shortage area.

591. Some schools and universities have the capability to provide an interactive classroom with Polycom video conferencing. The Polycom is usually used for a small group visiting back and forth. This technology is continually improving, but technology is not as good as actually being immersed in the country.

592. An interactive classroom is a larger group that can provide distance-learning programs. An example would be a class from your school visiting with a class in another country through the interactive program. The students can have a discussion, and the class may be taped to be used for discussion and viewing in class the next day.

593. Opportunities to travel and learn in another country will bring a whole new perspective to your work and enhance your knowledge base. It will expand your cultural competency and in turn will enrich your classroom. You will have a deeper empathy for your students if you go to a country where you are experiencing a language barrier similar to the one that they experience.

594. Go to an authentic restaurant of a different culture, and try the various foods your students have experienced in their country. Consider the possibility taking your class to the restaurant after you have had a good experience. This would be an expense for your students, so take that into consideration.

595. Familiarize yourself with the customs and holidays of your student's religions. Mark the holidays on the classroom calendar so you can recognize the celebrations.

596. Check on the Internet for cultural issues for all of the languages you have in your class. There are different rules and expectations in every culture. It is important to have an understanding of the rules and expectations of your students' cultures, especially to build relationships with the families. You do not want to offend them, just as they do not want to offend you.

597. Contact book companies and ask to review multicultural books from their company. Be cautious that the information is reputable and correct.

8.
Students with Special Needs

598. Remember that you do not get to select your students. They may have chosen you or your class, or the school may have assigned them to you. When they show up in your class, you have the responsibility to teach them. They may be gifted, talented, or academically challenged.

599. Familiarize yourself with the rules and procedures for seeking assistance from outside resources to meet the needs of special education students in your class. Also familiarize yourself with the rules and procedures for providing information about the student to outside sources.

600. Take an inventory of your beliefs about special education. They may contain biases that could affect your relationship with students and special education teachers. Realize that you will most likely have special needs students in your classes. Talk to the special education director or the principal about how the school provides for the needs of the identified students.

601. Introduce yourself to the special education teacher. If you are the special education teacher, introduce yourself to the general education teacher. You will be working very closely together, so take the time to get to know each other. Be sure to discuss classroom expectations, student expectations, and expectations of each other before the year begins.

602. You are responsible for all of the students in your classroom. Most of the special needs students will be identified with learning disabilities (LD). Students with learning disabilities will be expected to succeed in mainstream settings. You will be responsible to follow their Individualized Education Plan (IEP), and provide the modifications to their lessons that will assist the students in learning. Special education students are not an "add-on" to your roster; they are a part of your class.

603. There are many different conditions that will identify a student as special needs, such as autism, ADD (Attention Deficit Disorder), Tourette's, and many others. If you have a student who is identified with a special need, ask the special education teacher for material that will help you better understand the need. Not only will you benefit from a deeper understanding, but you will be better equipped to help your students.

604. Do not assume that all students in special education are mentally handicapped. For example, a student who is visually impaired, a student with Tourette's, or a student with ADD, may have a high IQ. Discuss individual students with the special education teacher to determine each student's academic capability.

605. Realize that the paperwork involved with a special needs student can be daunting. You will be keeping records and documentation, and the special education teacher will also be keeping documentation. This can be overwhelming and frustrating at times. Try to be as organized and methodical in your approach to record keeping as possible.

606. Even if you are not a special education teacher, know and use the legal terminology in special education such as Individualized Education Plan (IEP), accommodations, modifications, assistive technology, inclusion, and consultative model.

607. Learn as much as you can about special education law and regulations. This is to your benefit as you begin teaching special needs students in the classroom. Through websites and various workshops, learn as much as possible about special needs students and their rights.

608. Understand that by law you must follow the special needs student's IEP. Know specifically what the accommodations and modifications are for special needs students and what you must do to meet their needs. You can be fined for not following the IEP.

609. Ask your administration how special needs programs are structured and what models are being followed in the school district. NCLB (No Child Left Behind) and IDEA (Individuals with Disabilities Education Act) address how special education programs need to be administered. Become familiar with the service page of the IEP.

610. Follow the guidelines of the special education department in your school. They will provide forms, charts, checklists, and other materials that will help you to document the progress of the student. Be methodical about the documentation including dates and times. All information is important when annual IEP meetings are called to discuss a student's progress.

611. Schools must provide the least restrictive environment for each individual student. This might include anything from a special program in the school to a plan for treatment at an off-site facility. As the classroom teacher, you will be involved with programs within your building. You will meet regularly with the special education team and parents to discuss the student progress toward full inclusion in your classroom.

612. There are many organizations and agencies to help you with meeting the needs of exceptional children. You can request materials from the following groups:

- Office of Special Education and Rehabilitation Services—(202) 205-8241
- The Council for Exceptional Children—1-800-CEC-READ
- ADHD Warehouse—1-800-233-9273
- National Research Center on the Gifted and Talented—(203) 486-4826
- For information about learning disabilities visit the LD website at http://www.Idonline.org

New Special Education Teachers

613. If you are a new special education teacher, find support among the other special education teachers in your district. When in doubt, find outside resources such as national organizations and other professionals in the field of education.

614. Know where your students place academically at the beginning of the school year. Review the goals set the previous year, and explore the extent to which students were served during the summer. Make sure that students are able to have access to the general education curriculum where and when appropriate.

615. Give the inclusion classroom teacher note cards (a different color for each special education student) with the student's goals and a list of the modifications needed. Work as a team to ensure the best possible education.

616. Teach your special needs students how to learn and study until the students become responsible for the skills:

- Organizing materials and information
- Self-monitoring
- Time management
- Tools for remembering information
- Taking notes

These skills need to be taught to all students and periodically reviewed. For special needs students, these are taught, retaught, and reviewed in smaller segments, perhaps over a longer period of time.

617. Be flexible as you work with regular education teachers. The culture of the special education process is changing with NCLB. Keep the teacher informed of not only national changes but state and district changes as well. Coach the teacher and provide assistance.

618. Look at the big picture, but focus your energies on working with the students who are under your guidance. If appropriate, work with your regular education teacher to try to incorporate some of your lessons into the mainstream classroom.

619. Find out what is available for support in your district and state. The more you know about outside resources and expertise, the more you can apply the knowledge as you help move the special needs student forward in his or her learning.

620. Stay up to date with new technology designed to assist students in their learning: Examples include new auditory devices for the hearing impaired, computers that attach to sensors to assist the mobility of students, and scanners that can read print and translate into an auditory tape.

621. Become acquainted with the various outside providers who will be working with students and what support services they will be providing. If possible, make appointments with them before school begins or whenever new services begin. These professionals may include juvenile justice system workers, behavior intervention specialists, and social workers.

622. Work as a team with the outside support providers. Collaboration is a key component that will help to strengthen the support that a child is receiving. Develop a plan of communication that will work for all parties involved, including families.

623. Search the Internet for education sites that house chat rooms for special education teachers. Because the identification of students' disabilities are so broad, you may have one student with a somewhat unique disability or characteristic. You may find other teachers who have had similar students in the classroom. Sharing information can open up or support many possibilities.

624. Be aware of who needs to attend IEP meetings. Come prepared to the meeting with your data documented and in readable form. Share the information and your professional opinions. Some meetings can be very emotional because it can be very difficult for families to accept the extent of a disability.

625. If you teach students who will transition to another school, plan for the transition with the regular education teacher, other educators, the students, and the parents. Begin in middle school preparing for the transitions from school to the workplace or to postsecondary education.

626. Keep in regular contact with the families of your students. If the students have severe learning problems, written notes home, emails, or phone messages on a daily basis will aid their caregivers by providing information about the school day. You will be working very closely with families.

627. Establish a system for getting work to students who are absent over a period of time. It is critical that learning stays on course during absences more than several days. Call or set a time to visit if appropriate. Showing that you care is very important to the student and to the parents.

628. Send home small increments of extended work with the student. Ask parents to work on specific skills to accelerate the student's learning process. This is most crucial during the summer months when special needs students should continue to review skills.

629. Do not do for your students what they can do for themselves. It is perfectly okay to help your students, but empower them with as much responsibility and opportunity as possible. In younger grades, teach them how to zip their coats and then have them *show* you how they zip their coats. With older students, show them how to use the digital camera and then have them demonstrate what they have learned.

630. Struggling students may need to have their tasks or assignments broken down into chunks. Teach them to read a passage and write down a few notes about what they learned.

631. In math you might assign ten problems instead of twenty problems. Have the student check with you for understanding before proceeding with the next ten problems. Know that you can make accommodations for the student.

Teaching Strategies and Special Needs Students

632. There are three reading levels for special education students:

- The independent reading level: the student is reading on his or her own without support from others.
- The instructional reading level: The student requires instruction (challenging but not frustrating).
- Frustration reading level: Even with assistance, the material is too difficult.

633. Listen and observe the student that seems to have no interest in anything. Be patient and respectful, even if the student shows no emotion. Develop routines to try to reach the student such as always saying good morning to the student or sincerely complimenting him or her on something.

634. Learn as much as you can about each special needs student, his or her background, and past achievement performance. In many situations the students have become frustrated and overwhelmed by school. Visit with prior teachers and parents about your concerns. Chances are the parents are experiencing some of the same frustrations that you are seeing in school.

635. Investigate your school's retention policies and procedures. There is very little research that supports repeating the same grade for another year. Consider every aspect of the decision to retain a student in the same grade for another year. Some questions to ask are: Will the program be the same in year two of the same grade? Will retention affect the child's self-esteem? Have there been ongoing conversations with the parents about the possibilities of retention?

636. Some of your students may be "pulled out" of class to receive special services. Work with the teacher to schedule the time for your student to be out of your classroom. Do not expect the student to make up what they are missing in your classroom.

637. It is your responsibility to make adaptations in the content areas in which students have special needs. An example would be to have the students read through a math story problem, then write and repeat back to you specifically what the story problem is asking the student to answer.

638. Math story problems should be relevant to the student and reflect everyday situations. Help students to visually see what the story problem is asking and write the question on paper. List the facts that are available in the story problem and help the student work from what they know to find the answer.

639. In math, accept that some students may have different ways to arrive at the same answer. Be open to how they solve problems, and learn from each other.

640. In reading, allow the students to read with peers and use books on tape. Teach them to summarize the information as they read, and ask them questions to guide them in their comprehension while they are reading.

641. When writing, allow the student to tape record their story or dictate their ideas to another person to scribe for them.

642. For assessment, have the test orally read to the student and divide the test into sections.

643. Individualize spelling lists so students can move at their own pace. Check for understanding of spelling by requesting they explain what the word is and use it correctly in a sentence.

644. Organization is a struggle for some students. When students are young, teach them to return an activity to its proper place before working on another activity. Work on this skill with older students by helping them organize their schedules, priorities, and assignments.

645. Determine how you will adapt and teach critical context for all of your students. Don't assume that students can just "pick up" the information presented. Check the IEP to ensure that you are following the plan for each of your special needs students.

646. Keep in mind simple modifications that can work for many students but in particular, students with learning disabilities. Many of these have been mentioned before but are worth reiterating:

- Model processes and strategies to use that will help students to practice and use over time.
- Present work in small segments. Students won't feel overwhelmed or rushed.
- Allow additional time for assignments and/or tests, if needed.
- Present information both auditorily and visually.
- Use graphic organizers to assist students as they read and write.
- Provide opportunities for extended practice and application.
- Most importantly, follow the IEP!

647. If a "one size does not fit all" approach to teaching does not meet the needs of all of your students, conduct a learning styles test. Group students according to their learning style, which is how they learn best, and offer different assignments depending on the students' learning styles. Instead of one writing assignment for a class of thirty, you may have four or five different ways that students can show off what they learned. Include the modifications for your special needs students in one of the groups. By grouping students in this manner, labeling will be minimized.

648. Reflect upon what you teach. Do all students need to know minute details about Spanish American War, or the travels of Odysseus, or the different bird species in a region? Your special needs students may not be able to remember details, facts, or relationships as well as other students. Their group may focus on a portion of the learning, a more practical part of the learning, or a more skills-based approach to the learning.

649. In any content area, have multilevel reading books for the students in your classroom. Enlist the help of volunteers to read books on tape or purchase books on tape to help your special needs students. Taped books and textbooks are an excellent learning tool for students.

650. Utilize appropriate and continual assessments in order to know your students' reading levels and what skills the students have mastered. Keep a checklist of skills mastered.

651. Use the Internet to look for information, suggestions, and ideas that will help you better understand the abilities of your students. Look for ways to motivate, impact, and assess students who may have one or more disabilities.

652. Set a time before school begins to meet with the special education teacher. You might also ask the student's teacher, school nurse, and counselors from the previous year to join you as you begin to prepare to meet the needs of the students in your class.

653. Collaborate with the special education teacher. Do not expect the special education teacher to "teach" the special needs students the content that you are responsible for in the classroom. The students that are on your roster are your students and you will be grading them. Consider the following:

- Set a time to meet
- Plan a lesson together
- Team-teach a lesson
- Share materials
- Review what the student data show and act accordingly

654. Establish a division of responsibilities for the regular education teacher and the special education teacher. The regular education teacher will develop the content. The special needs teacher can provide assistance with the strategies, modifications, accommodations, and other requirements that the student(s) need.

655. You may also be working with a paraeducator in your room who is assigned as a "one-on-one" with a student or a small group. Meet with the special education teacher and the paraeducator on a regular basis to collaborate on student progress. You need to keep communication open at all times. Working as a team will have huge implications on the success of the special needs student.

656. During the meeting with the special education teacher and the paraeducator, review your classroom management plan, curriculum, and instructional techniques. Listen to their ideas as you craft a plan to work collaboratively in the classroom to meet the needs of the student(s).

657. Paraeducators are not licensed teachers but they have an acute sense of a student's habits, likes/dislikes, and personality traits. Respect their knowledge. Work together to impact student achievement.

658. Ask the special education teacher to teach instructional strategies and techniques that will benefit all students. Their background training will provide your students with multiple ways to learn.

659. At any time, several educational consultants might be in your room working with various students, observing students, or assisting students. Be welcoming and inviting. They are there to support students, not evaluate you.

660. Special education teachers are adept at implementing new strategies, different programs, and various approaches to assist students with their learning. Be flexible and able to adapt to the changes in a student's learning process.

661. Check to see if your school has "child study" teams that will meet to bring all of the people together for the purpose of discussion about meeting the needs of a student. If you have the student in your class, you will be asked for input and documentation on what you have done in your classroom to meet the needs of the student.

662. Child study teams usually consist of all of the teachers that teach the student, the parent/guardian, and an administrator. When you meet as a child study team, be prepared with evidence of the student's performance. Evidence would include test results, a sampling of their work, and any other documentation that will help tell the story related to the issue you are reviewing.

663. After the team meets and there has been documentation from the staff, they may write an IEP—Individual Educational Plan. The IEP will be the plan that everyone will participate in to help the student meet success. The IEP will include the present level of performance and any issues that may affect the performance of the student. There will be a date of review established and at that time you will be expected to again provide the documentation of your evidence of work with the student to meet the goals. Do not hesitate to call another meeting if you feel progress is in jeopardy.

664. Read the student's school health records and check attendance. Visit with the counselor and school nurse. If the student has not had a complete physical, involve the school nurse and seek his or her advice on school procedures for recommending health physicals for the student.

665. The school nurses often do hearing and vision screenings. Make sure your students participate in the free screenings. These are only screenings, however, and will not detect everything that may be hindering learning regarding vision and hearing.

666. Some students may need to leave your room to take "meds" (medication). The school nurse is generally the only person who can dispense medication to a student. Many of the special needs students are on medication and will need monitoring from you to ensure they receive their medication on time.

667. Be aware that some parents will pay money to resources outside of the school to evaluate their child. If the parent should share this information with you, consider the source and make every attempt to use the information to assist both you and the family to increase the academic performance of the student.

9.

Reach out to Parents and the Community

668. Communication is one of the most important responsibilities of being a teacher. You're responsible for not only communicating with your students, but also with the administration, community, and parents. Positive and constant communication is key to a successful career in education.

669. Send handwritten thank-you notes, not an email or voice message, but an actual card expressing your gratitude for support or volunteer time from a parent or community member.

670. Attend funerals or visitations of any student's family member if possible. If you are unable to attend, send a sympathy card to express your condolences.

671. Volunteer to chaperone dances, assist at plays and concerts, and take tickets at events. You may not be paid monetarily, but you may have the opportunity to get to know your students and colleagues on a personal level and enjoy an area other than the academics of your school.

672. Be creative and innovative. Ask a group of teachers to help develop a parent's university that will help parents understand how to assist their children with their homework and other issues. Invite guest speakers to discuss related social, emotional, and physical development issues. Partner with community agencies and other educational programs in the community.

673. Confidentiality is important in every aspect of your work. Do not engage in gossip about your students or their families outside of school or worse, with other students and their families. Refrain from gossiping or tattling about colleagues as well.

674. Answer all correspondence in a timely fashion. Parents, administrators, students, and colleagues will ask you questions. Don't wait; act immediately. If you do not know the answer, inform them that you do not know but would be willing to investigate.

Get Involved in the Community

675. If families of your students invite you to special events or celebrations, consider the appropriateness, and graciously acknowledge the generous invitation with a phone call or note. If it seems appropriate to attend, make a brief appearance.

676. Be loyal by supporting businesses that your students' families own. They are supporting you by sending their children to your school.

677. Wear the school colors and school logo whenever appropriate. You will feel a sense of belonging and it reflects support for your school.

678. Register to vote where you live so you can vote in school elections and for educational funding that will impact your work.

679. If you are a band teacher you have the opportunity to invite parents and community members to form an alumni or community band to perform at school events. They can perform with your students or alone. Do this to demonstrate to your students that playing a musical instrument can be a life skill and to recognize the talents of your community.

680. If you are the technology director, help your students plan a tech course for adults in the community. It will sharpen the student's skills to teach these skills to someone else, as well as keep community members and parents aware of ever-changing technology in the schools.

681. Contact your local media when your students are working on projects, planning special events, or practicing for a performance. They will need advance notice of your request to plan for the availability of a reporter and photographer. Provide a summary of the event so there is no confusion on what the purpose of the activity is at the school. Media coverage is powerful, and you do not want to neglect details when requesting free coverage.

682. If you've invited the media to an event, be sure you have a release form signed by the parents/guardians to have their child's picture taken and permission to publish. This can be done at school registration. Be sure to review that information so if there are any students that do not have that release form, you are sensitive to that issue.

683. Have the media email you any pictures they are going to use, to check for correct spelling of names, and so you are also assured that the students pictured have granted permission. Cut out any media highlights regarding your school or your students, and post them on a bulletin board in your classroom.

684. Radio stations also feature students and their events. Have your student write the who, what, where, and when information to share with the audience. Always practice with students a number of times before reading on the radio. Coach the student to read the information with expression and clarity.

685. Bring the school to your community. Showcase the talents of your student as they present vocal or instrumental solos and group ensembles. Ask if your groups can perform at the nursing homes, community organizations, or at local businesses. This will give the students an opportunity to practice in front of a smaller audience where ratings are not important.

686. Learn about opportunities for students to present and articulate their ideas. Competitions such as mock trials, science fairs, health fairs, math counts, invention convention, and history day, are a few events that provide structure for students to learn how to present what they have learned. There is usually a local, state, and national competition. Preparations for the competitions are often after school, and parents or community volunteers may serve as the coaches with the guidance of teachers or administration.

687. Send singing valentines from the school's vocal music department to businesses in the community that support the school. This could be three or four small groups of vocalists willing to participate in this project during study hall or music class period. Be sure to follow the school field trip policies when taking the students off-campus. Students must have signed permission slips.

688. Acknowledge people and organizations that help you teach your students. Students can present them with a certificate of appreciation or recognition.

689. Become active in your community by joining an organization that works for the betterment of the community. You will meet people outside of the school workplace and connect with people that support the school.

690. Ask students to send thank-you notes to people and organizations in the community that support the school and their activities. This is a powerful form of communication that can have lasting effects and promote good will. Students can also get practical writing experience.

Foster Positive Relationships with Colleagues

691. Invest time in developing a good working relationship with your administrator. The more the administrator knows about your philosophies and how you teach, the more the administrator is likely to support you during the year.

692. Principals tend to be very busy. Find out from other teachers or from the administrator the best way to communicate with him or her. Is it face-to-face in the hallway or cafeteria, by making an appointment, sending an email, or leaving a phone message? Knowing these things helps to build a stronger relationship.

693. Refrain from being negative about the administration in front of your colleagues or your students. It is unprofessional and doesn't speak well for you. Always try to keep the conversation positive.

694. If you have a complaint or a frustration to share, keep your wits about you as you converse with the principal. Your administrator traditionally has seen and heard a great deal of stories. He or she understands and probably has had the same experience with the same student, parent, or colleague.

695. Communicate with your administrator about something positive that has happened in your classroom. Principals sometimes only hear about problems. Send a "good news note" to your principal.

696. Offer to host a faculty meeting in your classroom and hope other teachers will follow your example. This will give everyone a chance to see your room. This is a great use of time for learning about your system and the good things taking place in the classrooms.

697. Show that you care about your colleagues by bringing treats to the teacher's lounge or workroom with a note that thanks them for the opportunity to work with such a talented group of teachers.

698. Volunteer to cover a class, take a recess duty, or supervise the lunchroom if a colleague needs to leave for an emergency. You may be in the same situation someday. You will also learn about what other people do in their positions in the school and have a better understanding of the system and the people that work in the system.

699. Ask colleagues to team up with you in writing a column for the local newspaper to let the community know what good things are happening in your school. Collaborate with other staff members to present the information about any new initiative. It is better to keep the community informed of any new programs prior to the implementation and keep them posted about the progress. They will be much more supportive if they are aware that there new things going on in your district to improve the student achievement.

700. Learn from your colleagues through weekly team planning and team teaching. Be a team player. Participate and do your part. Collaboration brings out the strengths and talents of every teacher.

701. Ask other educators for ideas, procedures, and other material that will help you in your work. Successful and happy teachers do not teach in isolation. Other teachers have valuable knowledge, wisdom, and experience that will assist us in making our job easier.

702. Review the academic history of each student. Make note of strengths and weaknesses, and apply that information as you work with your students. Request to have professional conversations with other teachers about the concerns you have for your student's academic or social performance.

Communicate with Parents

703. Foster positive relationships with parents/guardians by ongoing communication through a variety of means:

- Letter of introduction welcoming your students to a new school year
- Weekly, monthly, or quarterly newsletters authored by the teacher
- Class newsletters written by the students
- Phone calls
- Email messages
- Letter to welcome transfer students to your classroom
- Teacher websites

704. When writing a letter of introduction to parents or guardians, include a short paragraph about your philosophy of teaching, a paragraph about your curriculum, and exciting units/activities that are planned. The one page letter can also include information about back-to-school night activities and an invitation for parents to attend. Consider attaching a sheet that asks for volunteers for chaperoning field trips and helping with class projects.

705. Use weekly, monthly, or quarterly newsletters to communicate with families. The newsletters are a great way to inform families about:

- Upcoming events and activities in the school
- Projects and other assignments due for class
- Information about hard subjects

Before sending the newsletter to families, ask your principal to review the newsletter. Always keep the principal informed about what is happening in your class.

706. In elementary grades, set a day to send home weekly letters to parents. Use this opportunity to send home extended learning activities for parents and students to work on together. Parents will be expecting the activities and any calendar information they will need for the next week. Have students return a confirmation that their parent or guardian received the letter. If you are not consistently hearing from the families, contact them directly by phone or make a home visit.

Parent-Teacher Conferences

707. Meeting parents/guardians for a parent-teacher conference may be very intimidating, but it is also very rewarding. You are working together to support the student, review his or her progress, and assist the student in achieving his or her goals. Be prepared before, during, and after the conference.

708. Take the time early in the school year to ask other teachers or the administration the following:

- How parent-teacher conferences are structured
- What the expectations for teachers are
- Who sets the schedules for the conferences
- What the format is for the conferences

709. Many schools conduct student-led conferences. If you are expected to facilitate student-run conferences, which places the responsibility on the student, begin to plan early and practice with the students.

710. As you prepare for conferences, be prepared with the following:
- Background information about the families
- Information about the student
- Specific projects and assignments that represent the student's work in a folder

711. Collect student work and place the work in a portfolio. The teacher can mandate some of the pieces that will be used and ask the student to choose the other pieces. Develop a list of points that the students need to address in the conference.

712. Allow students to select some of the work that they want parents/guardians to view. You are providing the student with choices and responsibility for the conferences. Students can reflect on their work by writing a short paragraph about what they have learned, if they are obtaining their long-term goals, and what they will change or keep the same about their work habits.

713. Practice the student-led conference with the students. The teacher models a conference and then pairs students who will practice their conference. The student takes charge of their learning by reporting to the parents/guardians.

714. If offering student-led parent-teacher conferences, make sure the parents/guardian are aware of the procedures so they are not expecting to attend the usual teacher-driven conferences.

715. If you schedule your own conferences or as a team, or if the office schedules conferences, build in a break time. You will welcome the time to stretch, walk around, get a quick snack, or take care of other necessities.

716. Arrange the area that you have been assigned for the conferences. This area may be in your room or in another assigned room, the cafeteria, or the gym. Wherever you are assigned, place yourself and the families away from the door or other teachers. The conversation is between you and the families—not the entire community. Show only the student's work. Print out a record of his or her work, grades, or points. Do not open your grade book with other students' grades listed. Confidentiality is important.

717. Wherever you are located for parent-teacher conferences, try to display student work samples, projects, or pictures. Arrange student folders according to conference time. Check that the table is clean and that the area around you is neat and orderly. Some parents find parent-teacher conferences to be daunting because of previous personal experiences at school. Provide a welcoming environment.

718. Keep in mind that first impressions are very important. Check your body language and ask yourself what message you are communicating to families. Be confident, and extend your hand as you greet the families. Smile, be cordial, and be inviting. First impressions will not be forgotten.

719. When families arrive at the conferences, escort them to the seating area. Use a table to display the student's work from the folder. Arrange four adult chairs on one side of the table with your chair turned toward the others to create a more open, welcoming environment. Refrain from using student desks. Some parents cannot fit in the desks and it can become very embarrassing when they struggle to get in or ask you for a chair.

720. Greet parents and introduce yourself if you have not met them previously. Tell them that you are pleased that they could attend. If you have some background knowledge of the family, you might ask a question such as "I understand that you moved to the area last year. I am new here also." Use ice breakers to set the tone of the conference.

721. Begin the parent-teacher conference with comments accenting the student's strengths. You might use the following examples. The child:

- Is motivated
- Is excited about being in school
- Enjoys working with classmates
- Is a diligent worker
- Completes assignments
- Follows directions
- Is focused on learning
- Finishes work on time

Parents/guardians want to hear positive comments about their child. Beginning the conferences this way helps to put parents at ease.

722. Explain clearly to parents/guardians academic and behavioral expectations and guidelines that have been established. Clearly state the academic policy for your class. Parents don't always know the expectations set by the teacher and/or students.

723. Review a handout that clearly explains class rules, expectations, and procedures. The more that parents know and understand about your classroom, the easier it will be to discuss their child's academic and behavioral performance.

724. In addition to communicating homework expectations, encourage parents to work with their child in specific areas that need attention. Give the parents a list of homework guidelines to follow.

725. After communicating positive accolades, focus on the goals set by the student. If there are areas for improvement, show the data that support those areas. Grading can be very subjective. Show how you grade and where improvement can be reached. Parents/guardians want to know what their child is capable of doing, what they are learning, and how you know they are learning.

726. Know how to interpret the standardized test scores that will need to be reported to parents/guardians. You may receive an empty graph that will need to be filled out or a computerized report. Know what you are talking about. Ask the counselor for an explanation.

727. In a data-driven educational environment, evaluate the student's progress by identifying what students need to know at their grade level. Identify the skills that may be lacking, discern how to address the needs through specific learning strategies, and finally develop an action plan that will record the action taken to address the needs and the results of those actions. Parents have a right to know how and what you are teaching, where their child ranks, and how you plan to close their child's achievement gap or how you will promote learning to gifted and talented children.

728. When addressing a problem, begin by asking the student or parent what they would do to improve the situation. Build on their input, but have some concrete ideas of your own before the meeting. If a meeting turns hostile, you should reschedule and inform your administrator. Be sure to follow up because unresolved conflict will only become more hostile.

729. If parents need to speak with you about other concerns they have and don't want the student to hear, ask the student to step outside the room for a few minutes. This is not an odd request because most parents are used to a parent-teacher conference without the child. Honor the request.

730. End the conference on a positive note. Summarize the main points that were talked about during the conference. If an action plan was established, reiterate the main points. If you need to write a contract, a discipline plan, or a homework completion plan, you need to reestablish the time lines and when you will be reporting again to the parents/guardians. Thank the parents/guardians for attending.

731. If parents/guardians do not attend conferences, contact them and try to set up another time that may be more convenient. If you do home visits, do not travel to the homes alone for legal and safety reasons.

732. If you meet with parents/guardians outside of regular school hours, alert your administrator to the time and date. Do not have meetings alone at night or early in the morning. At least alert the school custodian that you are in the building and that you are meeting with someone.

733. As angry or frustrated as you might be with a parent or guardian, do not make it personal. The reality is some parents will act in the best interest of their children, and some won't. You are not there to pass judgment.

10.
Maintaining Professionalism

734. Invest yourself in your business—the business of educating students to be good stewards, outstanding citizens, and lifelong learners. Know that this is the most important career. What you teach students will greatly impact their lives.

735. Check your beliefs about education regularly. Ask yourself why you want to be a teacher. If it's because you love to work with kids, assess how you are doing. If it's just a job, find ways to make it more meaningful for you and your students.

736. Find the best practices in books and journal articles that base their findings on what research tells us is the best way to impact student learning. This will strengthen your educational foundation, the lessons you develop, and student achievement.

737. Get letters of recommendation from teachers you work with and the principal. If you wait until you're interviewing for a new job, you will be scrambling to ask people to write and send the letters to potential employers.

738. When offered a contract for the next year, assess whether you like the school and the staff. Are you supported by the administration? Do you know the content for the grade you teach? Do you like the location? Do you feel safe? If most of the answers are positive, sign your contract for another year.

739. Teach students first. Be student-centered in every decision that you make. Students are the reason why you are in education. Be careful not to fall into the trap of focusing on content first and students second.

740. Post your schedule by the door so you and your students can be found easily if your class has gone to lunch or the library. Don't expect people to chase after you.

Appropriate Behavior Begins with You

741. If you express a bias for working with students of a particular race, religion, or gender, students will notice this even if you think it's not obvious. Word will spread and it is very difficult to change perceptions or the way students think about you.

742. Shake a bad mood before entering the classroom. Snapping at the students is not the best way to begin your day or a class. You may be upset about the quality of the projects that you graded the night before, but instead of getting angry, focus on how you're going to improve your students' performance.

743. Submit work on time. If reports, lesson plans, or forms are due in the office, to another teacher, to the principal, or the central office, get them to the designated person ahead of time if possible. You are setting an example to your students.

744. Perform assigned duties as directed by the administration. If you have to take tickets at a concert or athletic event, be there on time with a good attitude. If you have a faculty meeting after school, make arrangements for child care (if needed) and transportation.

745. Your opinions about political educational issues should be directed to your state representatives. These opinions and the actions you take are important, but they don't belong in the classroom.

746. Accept responsibility for your actions if you make an error. Trying to get out of a messy situation only magnifies the problem. Own up to it, and work out a solution. Whether it is with a colleague, a parent, or a student, remain professional in your words and actions.

747. Remember that respect is mutual. If you are interacting with a student by addressing him or her by name, taking interest in what they do, and staying calm through difficult situations, you are demonstrating respect for the student.

748. If you have misspoken or if your assumptions were wrong, apologize to your students or colleagues. Be frank, be brief, and be sincere. Students and adults will appreciate your honesty and your courage.

749. Accept personal responsibility for each of your students. You are their teacher and it is your responsibility and your job to teach all of your students using various strategies. Know that an education is for life.

750. Understand that you may be asked to teach more than the grade or content area assigned to you. You will need to teach conflict mediation skills, conduct mini-lessons on alcohol and drug abuse, and work on study skills. More "other" curriculum is being adopted by the legislature and mandated by schools to teach.

751. Always use proper grammar when speaking and writing. Double negatives and slang phrases are not appropriate for classroom use. A teacher wouldn't teach the wrong subject matter. The same applies for language usage.

752. Learn ways to build trusting relationships between school, community, and families. Trust takes time and credibility. You work on both in order to influence learning. You build trust through communication, and by keeping your word.

753. Pay attention to what is happening in the school. Read the announcements, listen to the intercom, and ask questions when confused or clarification is needed.

754. Handle mail once. Find a place to put catalogues (you will receive many). Immediately discard any mail that is perceived to be unusable. Respond that day to important information then toss or file.

Things to Watch out For!

755. Beware of alliances that form within the school and attaching yourself to one group of teachers. This can be detrimental if you do not talk to other teachers, sit with one group of teachers, and become a clique.

756. Find out what your school's policy is on holiday celebrations and use of religious symbols. The school may have a policy, an unwritten rule, or may not address this issue. Remember that your students come from many backgrounds. Honor the diversity.

757. Remember that religion is a personal choice. Keep it to yourself and out of the classroom if you are teaching in a public school. If you need to pray during the day, pray during your break or at lunch. Don't ask your students to pray with you. This is a violation of separation between church and state.

758. If you are sick, stay home. But if you think you just need a day off, take a personal day. Don't try to cheat the system. Be honest with yourself and the school district. They keep a record of personal days and sick days.

759. Don't ignore possible substance abuse problems. Consult with the counselor or at-risk coordinator immediately if you suspect buying, selling, or taking of illegal or prescription drugs.

760. If you are a young high school teacher, be aware of your age in comparison with your students. Be responsible for you actions and relationships you have with students. Address any issues before they turn into potential problems.

Self-Improvement Is Important

761. Look for books and journal articles that support what you are doing in the classroom and can offer more strategies and techniques to use in the classroom. You can find professional reading materials in your school library. If you cannot find reading materials, ask where the professional library is located in your school.

762. Observe other teachers not only formally but informally as well. How do they conduct themselves in the hallway, at lunch, during bus duty, or with parents? What can you learn from these observations? How will your students benefit? What techniques can you adopt for your classroom? When you focus solely on your own classroom, you have no one to emulate or learn new ideas from.

763. During a teacher evaluation conference, discuss what areas of improvement you need to work on. Devise a plan that will address these areas and keep data that show you have addressed the areas. Don't wait for the administrator to tell you what he or she thinks. Either discuss together or take the initiative to do it on your own.

764. Videotape a lesson that you are teaching at least twice a year. Critique the major components of the lesson. Note the area of improvement that is needed. Develop a plan to address these areas. Be sure to check with your administration about the school's policy on videotaping.

765. Do not hide your passion for teaching or your passion for the subject matter. Show your excitement. This excitement is contagious and translates into student enthusiasm, which can be a motivational tool.

766. Model whatever it takes to affect student achievement. In other words, try a variety of ways to connect with your students. Write positive notes when students gain points on tests, call parents with good news about behavior, and keep encouraging students on a daily basis.

767. Demonstrate how knowledge is integrated in life. Bring in speakers who can address how important school was to them. Bring in former students who struggled and can talk about the challenges of finding a job. Bring in workers who can talk about the need for technical skills. Their testimonials will be more effective than what is learned from a book.

768. The Internet is a valuable resource. Use it to search for projects, information, lesson plans, strategies, and other materials that can be used in class. Utilize search engines to guide your search.

769. Find ways for your class to take virtual field trips. This can be an inexpensive way to provide an opportunity for students to experience learning in a real-time situation. Investigate how you can join an expedition to Alaska, explore the rain forest, or discover the problem of acid rain.

770. Begin service projects with your students. Students need to participate in community linked service projects to foster a relationship with their community or future communities. The benefits include a spirit of working together for the common good, a sense of accomplishment, and a sense of belonging.

771. Allow students to help plan events in the classroom, service learning projects, and field trips. The students have more ownership and will gain additional experiences as they plan and work together.

772. Keep a file of special projects your class did for the year. This will help you remember the highs and the lows of the year. Review your portfolio before the next year to revise things that worked and areas that need improvement.

773. Read the latest journal articles in your area of teaching. The articles provide strategies and techniques you might apply to your area. Add any ideas to your folder of good teaching practices.

774. Realize the workplace is changing rapidly and that you are preparing students for careers that may not have been developed yet. Teach students how to develop thinking skills that will transfer to any job or situation. Teach a thinking strategy during a unit where a student can practice the skill until mastery has been achieved by demonstration.

775. Expand your knowledge about areas that are indirectly related to what you teach. This information will translate into a deeper understanding of the concept, and at some point may apply to other subject areas.

776. Grab opportunities that will expand your horizons such as course tours of countries throughout the world. Show your students that many experiences come from traveling to other countries and experiencing different cultures. Universities often offer inexpensive trips for college credit.

777. Understand the role that emotions play in learning. If emotions and learning go hand in hand, then a deeper understanding of the interplay must be recognized in order for learning to exist in the classroom. Students remember the scared feeling when reading a passage from a haunting short story or the thrill of a bull's-eye in archery during PE. Emotions link you to learning through experience.

778. Ask your administrator if you can visit other schools to discover what other teachers are doing to enhance student achievement. Prepare questions before you go. Maximize your time and learning by visiting several schools. Use what applies to your classroom.

779. Be willing to pilot new material if it fits the classroom curriculum. You will gain knowledge from the material and experience from facilitating student learning. You will be asked to provide your insights and data collection pertaining to the new material.

780. Begin planning for the next school year every day. Make notes about changes and improvements in your lessons, carefully store bulletin board material for next year, attend conferences, and take classes that provide strategies to impact learning. Don't wait until the day before school to get ready. Do this throughout the school year, and you won't be in a panic in August.

Attending Conferences and Workshops

781. When you are attending a class, a professional development course, a workshop, or a conference, go with a good attitude and be ready to learn. Although you may want to bring papers to correct or material to read, stay focused on the workshop. As an active participant you will gain more by asking questions or providing comments. Show the instructor the same respect that you expect from your students.

782. If the class, workshop, or conference was not particularly helpful in regards to extending your learning, provide constructive feedback to the instructor or presenter. Be specific when writing your comments.

783. To help make it through a day-long presentation at a workshop, bring water and snacks. Usually coffee, tea, and rolls are provided, but high-energy food will give you the lift you need for the duration of the session.

784. Even if you disagree with the message, keep an open mind during a workshop or conference. Watch your body language and body posture. Listen intently, and make eye contact with all parties involved. Don't let your mind wander.

785. If you are uncomfortable speaking in front of large groups, take a public speaking course, join Toastmasters International, or register for assertiveness training. The tips and suggestions that you learn will help you to become more assertive and articulate in your delivery of daily lessons, during meetings, and in general conversation.

786. Be an active participant in meetings. Listen intently, and voice your opinion where appropriate. Refrain from grading papers.

Maintain Professionalism at School

787. When shopping for clothes, remember that all eyes are on you. Students see everything that is wrong and out of place and they are not afraid to tell you. Make sure that your clothes fit appropriately. Women, beware of tight fitting pants, low-cut tops, and short skirts. Men, keep clothes wrinkle-free.

788. Before you leave the house, check yourself in the mirror. Look for food on the face, nose residue, makeup that smeared, or a zipper that is unzipped. A ten-second look will alleviate any potential embarrassment that might be caused because you forgot several buttons or because your skirt is tucked in your panty hose.

789. Be on time to school in the morning, and for all meetings and conferences. In fact, being early helps to de-stress you so that you can gather your thoughts. Colleagues and students will notice your promptness.

790. Follow the school rules and policies of the district even if some don't quite make sense to you. You are an employee of the school district and need to abide by the guidelines.

791. Use the school telephone for school business only. Calling family and friends to chat during business hours is unprofessional. Remember to keep your cell phone off, on vibrate, or at home.

792. Be professional with colleagues even if they are rude to you, flirt with you, or are intimidating. Don't be rude in return, and don't flirt in return. You are in the business of educating students; don't lower your standards.

793. Don't bad-mouth your students to other teachers. Realize that you are a professional. No matter how frustrated you are, try to solve the problems that are developing without demeaning a student. Look for solutions instead.

794. Computers are the property of the school and are not personal property. A computer has a memory that can be retrieved. Use it only for school business.

795. Refrain from sending personal emails from your school email account. Keep your personal world private from your world as an educator. You have little control over an email that a friend has sent with negative, vulgar remarks or pictures that are sent as a joke. Delete the inappropriate email immediately.

You Always Represent the School— Even on Your Own Time

796. When a parent stops you in public and asks about his or her child, tell them you will call them to talk about their child or ask if they will come to school. In smaller communities it is difficult to keep conversations private. A better time and place needs to be considered.

797. Find out what the official dress code calls for at your school. The terminology is usually vague. Ask several teachers, the secretaries, and the administrator. Schools generally have more of an unwritten dress code. If the building is not air-conditioned during the hotter months, can you wear shorts? Are you allowed to wear sneakers? Can you wear jeans on Friday? You will want to dress within the code—written and unwritten.

798. Remember that all eyes from the community are on you if you live in a small urban or rural area. Keep in mind that you live in a fish bowl. Conduct yourself in a professional manner at all times. You are still a teacher, even if it is after 3:00 p.m.

799. Think before you buy liquor or cigarettes at a grocery or convenience store where your students work. Although it is legal for you, students will take the opportunity to talk about you to their friends. You need to be a role model. If you need to, buy your liquor outside of the district.

800. Maintain confidentiality with school-related business. Many of the occurrences at school are totally unrelated to what you are doing in the classroom. You generally have secondhand information. Keep the information to yourself instead of telling the community.

801. Get into the habit of using appropriate language in and out of school. Keep street language, slang, and swearwords out of your vocabulary.

802. Don't get involved in conversations about religion, politics, or other hot-button issues if you have a vested interest. Also be aware of inappropriate comments, offensive ideas, and distasteful language.

803. Schools are small and gossip can run rampant both within the school and the community. Spreading gossip is detrimental to you and hurtful for others involved. Avoid gossip at all costs.

11.

Personal Management

804. Periodically give your mind a break. A brief mental vacation will keep you alert and engaged for longer stretches of time. Think about a personal goal you have. Close your eyes and visualize that you are some place else other than the demands of the classroom.

805. Establish a smooth school preparation routine. When things are organized you are in a better frame of mind to begin the day with students. Have your schoolbag packed and by the door. If you take your lunch, make it the night before.

806. Stay focused during the workweek by staying on a school schedule and regular sleeping and eating routine. Good planning time can be wasted if you do not stay focused on your work.

807. Ask for help when you need it. Everyone needs assistance at some time. You will feel much better when you are on the right track.

808. Keep breath mints handy. After talking with students for a period of time, you need to freshen your breath.

809. During class, provide stretch breaks. If students are sitting for longer periods of time, ask the students to stand for a stretch break. The blood will be forced to move to the brain. Get up and stretch with them—you also may need a break.

810. Do not be afraid to say no to volunteer requests if you just do not have the time available. This may take some practice, but you need to know your limitations. A schedule that is full does not have room for extras.

811. Know when you are the most productive during the day. Maximize this time by focusing on the long list of things that need to be accomplished.

812. Reevaluate how you are using the twenty-four hours in a day. Working smarter will help you to cope with the deluge of demands on your time.

813. Set time limits for tasks. It is easy to get caught up in a project and spend too much time stewing and fretting over the small details.

814. Prioritize all of your routines, activities, and lists in your mind. Know what needs to be accomplished today, tomorrow, and in the near future. This only needs to take a little forward thinking.

815. Do the job you are dreading the most first. Get that job out of the way, and go immediately to the next job.

816. Plan the night before what you will wear to school. Have the clothes ready to wear. This saves time in the morning when time is very valuable!

817. Make a list every night of what you need to do the next day, and be sure to check the list and cross off tasks after you accomplish each one. This helps you manage your time and your schedule.

Dealing with Stress

818. Try to keep stress at a minimum. Nothing is more important than your health. Most likely your school will have a wellness program and if not, create one in your classroom. You could have your students create a walking path. The math students could calculate out a mile walk.

819. Be aware of signs of stress in yourself and your students. The signs of stress are universal. Changes in sleeping, eating, and work habits are signs of stress. Mood swings, sudden outbursts, and crying are all signs of stress and should not be ignored.

820. By modeling for your students how you handle stress, you will be showing them ways to handle their own stress. Students will have a clearer mind and will be able to learn if they can find ways to deal with stress.

821. Share research regarding yoga, walking, breathing exercises, and meditation. Invite expert speakers that have been cleared through your school to the classroom to discuss the areas of stress management.

822. Keep soft music playing in the background during your prep period. If you have students in the room during your prep time, you may want to use headphones so as not to disturb anyone. Research has found that playing classical music stimulates the brain.

823. Plan ahead, if possible, to help alleviate "crunch time" planning. Stress will be lessened and you will have the energy to teach the lesson.

Exercise and Nutrition

824. Talk about the healthy foods you like and eat on a regular basis. Students, who aren't taught food nutrition in the home need to hear how to live a healthy lifestyle from teachers. If you are not the best person to talk about healthy diets, invite experts from the hospital who are trained dieticians.

825. Exercise at least three days per week, if not more. Exercise keeps your body healthy and sends much needed oxygen to the brain to keep it healthy as well.

826. Schedule time to exercise. Keep this a priority. If mentally you don't think of exercising as a priority, you will find all types of excuses.

827. Find a friend to exercise or workout with after school. The time goes fast and you may be able to talk about any frustration that you're feeling and feel much better when you enter your home.

828. Participate in the food service program as often as your can. This is a salute to the school cooks. The price is usually low and you can observe your students in a social setting.

829. Watch what you eat. It is surprising how adults react to different foods. Know your own body and how it reacts to various foods. For example, stay away from foods that are too stimulating (caffeine), or foods that zap the body of needed nourishment.

830. Watch how much you snack on in the teacher's lounge. It's easy to eat the snacks but it is not easy to stay awake later or drop the pounds down the road.

831. Drink lots of fluids. You need to keep plenty of liquids in your body, or you begin to feel sluggish and tired. Working with students of all ages takes an abundance of energy!

832. Stop and think before you grab another cup of coffee, can of soda, or candy bar. Although they are quick and easy stimulants, the fast energy lift diminishes quickly, leaving the body drained.

833. Buy a box of crackers or granola bars to have in your desk in case you miss breakfast or do not have time for lunch. Be sure to not leave the food in your desk or closets over the vacations as it might attract insects.

834. Students need nourishment to do well in school. Many schools offer the breakfast program for a nominal fee to their staff and students. School breakfast can be a great social way to begin the school day.

835. If you think your students need snacks during the day, you may want to visit with the cooks or parents about possibly providing snacks. It is a great benefit for your students. Suggest that parents take turns providing the snacks.

836. During your planning time, do exercises at your desk that will help to send oxygen to the brain and extremities. Do deep breathing exercises or chair exercises such as leg lifts. You will feel energized and will be able to better teach the students the remainder of the day.

837. Teach students the benefits of a healthy lifestyle when the topic fits the curriculum. Many students may know about the healthy tips, but do not see relevance in their lives at their age.

Protect Yourself from Getting Sick

838. Wash your hands every chance that you get, or use a hand cleansing gel to keep flu and cold germs away. Germs permeate a school and are found everywhere.

839. Keep disinfectant supplies available, but out of student reach and behind closed doors. During cold and flu season, you will need the cleaning agents to keep the germs at bay.

840. Keep plastic gloves available for cleaning and blood borne cleanups. Most school districts provide these supplies. Ask the office if you can obtain the gloves.

841. Beware of student allergies. Your students may have reactions to cleaning supplies. Check before you ask them to clean desks or the room.

842. Remember to take the necessary precautions every cold and flu season. An ounce of prevention is worthwhile every day in the classroom. Keep tissues on hand for yourself and your students. Keep hand sanitizer at your desk.

843. If possible get a flu shot. Sometimes the school or the public health office will provide them at school for a nominal fee.

844. Establish that all students have their own water bottle with their name on it if they are participating in sports. They may have to provide their own, but it is better than sharing the colds and flu virus.

845. Remind students to wash their hands when they go to the restroom. If you say it often enough, students will remember to wash off the germs every time.

846. Ask your custodian to place signs in the restroom that remind students not to put things in the toilets. It will only take one time of embarrassment to have the bathroom closed for repair or the plumber working on a clogged pipe.

847. Take multivitamins to keep your immune system in tip-top shape. Vitamins also help your body stay alert.

848. Bring your own coffee cup to school. This guarantees that you're always drinking out of a cup that you've washed yourself.

Maintain a Life Outside of School

849. Keep your school life and your home life in balance. Some days you will spend more time on the job; other days you may have to ask to leave early for doctor's appointments, your children's games, or travel time to take a class. You will be happier if you feel like you are still having time to enjoy your family.

850. Schedule time for yourself. Time for yourself is one of the best stress relievers according to experts. Until you realize how much better you feel, you are passing up the best and cheapest therapy possible.

851. Use self-talk to assist you in dealing with the stressful situations at school. When in doubt, talk your way through a situation. This saves you from building up resentment, pity, and more stress later.

852. Your schedule during the school year is demanding. Do not expect perfection out of yourself all of the time during the school year. Plan some personal projects for days that you have free. Projects might be the things you want to get done, but you always put your students and schoolwork first.

853. Continue to stay in contact with relatives and friends. It is too easy to become engulfed in teaching. Friendships are lifelines of support that promote your well-being.

854. Find someone outside of teaching who will serve as your confidante. Venting to someone in the system might get back to the student or your administration and be interpreted the wrong way.

855. Develop interests and hobbies outside of school. If you can only talk about work related subjects, you may become a one-dimensional conversationalist, which translates into dull.

856. Encourage students to gather a list of activities to do outside of school. So much emphasis is placed on school athletics but not all students have the resources or desire to play an organized sport. Open their learning to other activities that will promote a healthy body and mind.

Remember to Have Fun!

857. Find humor in the classroom. Too often teachers are afraid to laugh at themselves. Have joke books available and read the comic strips. Encourage your students to share appropriate jokes and cartoons with the class.

858. Make learning fun for you and your students. If you are bored, the students certainly will be also. Talk with enthusiasm, and listen with interest to your students.

859. Relax and enjoy your job. Getting worked up over every little detail or happening will cause more problems for you, your students, and others involved in their learning.

860. If your students are involved in performances, attend them. Support your students with encouragement and praise.

861. If you're having a bad day, reflect on the students you have had in your class. Savor the moments you remember when you made a difference in their learning. You may find happiness in the memory.

862. Motivating students is a challenge you will face as a teacher. Never give up, like the unmotivated student already has. The student needs to know someone cares and believes that they can be successful.

863. Take a Friday and make it a "fun learning day" for all. Sturdy boxes have many uses in your classroom, especially boxes with handles. The younger grades like to build houses with boxes of any size and the older grades can use boxes for their plays or for school dances. Plan accordingly, and you and your class will be refreshed and can catch up on Monday.

864. Keep a list of people who are knowledgeable, available, and stimulating and use this human wealth to provide more learning. Your school or community should have a list of volunteers that have an expertise and are willing to share their knowledge with the students. Again, speakers need office approval so visit with the administration before inviting people into the building to speak to your class.

Managing Your Finances

865. Design a budget of your fixed monthly expenses and your monthly salary. Decide what your financial goals are, and spend and save accordingly.

866. Consider experiences that enrich your life like sharing a meal with a friend, watching a ballgame on television with others, or taking a walk with a friend. These don't cost a fortune and can allow you to socialize with others.

867. Do not worry about how your housing or the car compares to the students. Ask yourself if your car is safe, clean, and dependable. Is your housing safe, clean, and accessible?

868. Collect your loose change in a container, and cash it in at the bank when the container is full. You will be surprised how much currency loose change can become.

869. Remember when friends are receiving holiday bonuses that you receive your bonuses from much greater things. The bonus includes students saying thank you, telling you that you are the best teacher, little notes and formal letters, and general job satisfaction.

870. Model for students how you found information that was free of charge. It never hurts to ask for something if you think it will improve the education for your students.

871. Take advantage of the school district's professional development opportunities that are free and will extend your learning. Students will benefit and you will also. Many schools have professional development plans written to align with their goals.

872. When you are interviewed you should ask what professional development opportunities are available and if the expense will be through you or the school. Many schools have grants that can only be used for improvement of instruction, but they are quite specific and can only be utilized in particular areas.

873. Keep personal business to yourself. Others don't have to hear about your money problems or social life—especially your students! Remember you are in a position of authority and you are not their best friend. Do not visit with students about things you would discuss with your friends or spouse.

874. Make personal appointments well in advance. You will not need to take precious learning time to visit the doctor, financial advisors, or attorneys during school.

875. Watch for sales—buy clothes, paper, supplies, books, and storage bins when the ads appear in the paper. Being thrifty is smart on a limited budget.

876. Save sturdy boxes with handles and lids to store your school supplies. Mark your name and the contents with a permanent marker. Teachers often are moved to a different classroom every year. Be prepared so you don't have to spend money on new boxes and moving supplies.

877. Bookstores and supply stores will often give a discount to teachers if they present their teacher ID or business card. Keep your professional identification in your billfold so you always have it with you should you see the perfect find for your classroom.

878. If you are going to a conference, check out hotels that provide special rates for educators. Some hotels will give special rates if you are employed by the public school system and the district has negotiated a lower rate for their staff.

879. If you are participating in educational events, such as museum programs, art shows, or musical performances, inquire about any educational discounts being offered to teachers.

880. Some districts will expect you to take tickets at school events and others might pay you for your time at the event. Regardless, you will probably have free admission to the school activities if you are helping with the programs.

881. It is your personal choice if you want to join the teacher association. You should visit with both members and non-members to learn about the benefits of joining so you know if membership is a good thing for you personally and professionally.

Managing Your Career

882. Take time to ascertain the benefits of your job. When the grass looks greener on the other side, take stock of what makes you happy in your job. You have tangible benefits such as a secure monthly paycheck, health insurance, holiday time off, and a summer vacation.

883. Make a list of the pros and cons of your job. If the negatives outnumber the positives, set the list aside and in a couple weeks reevaluate. You can either find the source of discontent or begin looking for new positions.

884. Frame your teacher's license and college diploma and hang them by your desk in your office, or in your classroom. They will serve as reminders that you have worked hard to accomplish graduation and licensure.

885. Maintain a professional file of your transcripts, grades, certificates of training, and a current passport. You want to be prepared for all opportunities. You will refer to this file your entire professional career when applying for positions, so do not discard.

886. Have a phone card or cell phone with you to use at school if you need to make personal calls during your break time. Workplaces will assign a code number to their employees if there is a need to call long-distance. If you're expecting a call from a prospective employer, let them know your schedule so they do not call you in the middle of teaching a class.

887. Always write your name and date on any correspondence. Create your own letterhead if necessary. This will ensure all correspondence regarding your career is neat, professional, and consistent.

888. Keep your resume updated every year and have your professional file current. As you meet people and think they would be a good reference, ask them to write a recommendation for you to place in your files.

889. Recommendation letters should be typed and current. Provide a self-addressed stamped envelope, and send a thank-you note to the person writing your recommendation.

890. If you transfer or leave your school building after the first year, stay in contact with your colleagues from your first year of teaching. You will always remember your first year of teaching. There is a bond from learning together.

891. Program cuts usually occur every year, and sometimes the last hired are the first to go. It is difficult not to take this personally, but it is usually just a matter of seniority and budget constraints.

892. Bring a few personal items to school that reflect your interest and hobbies. Even if you know you're only going to stay at your current school for a year, you owe it to yourself and your students to make a full commitment for that year. Set up as though you're planning to stay awhile—you may surprise yourself at the end of the year!

12.
Safety in Schools

893. Safety is of utmost importance in all schools. Whether you spend your career in one school or five, or at elementary or high school levels, the biggest responsibility of being a teacher is to ensure that your students are kept safe while under your watch.

894. Do you feel safe? Do you feel welcomed? Those are two questions that need to be asked about the culture of your school and your classroom. If students respond that they do not feel safe or they do not feel welcomed, you have a responsibility to find out why and do something.

895. Observe your students and their interactions with others. Listen to what the students are saying to each other. The information will help you create the safe and welcoming atmosphere you want in your school and classroom.

896. Keep your school keys with you at all times on a key chain that is not obvious. Never keep them on top of your desk. Instead, keep them in a safe and secure place. You are responsible for the keys and if they are lost or stolen you may have to pay for the rekeying of the building.

897. Every school has sexual and harassment policies in the official school handbook. Invite the school counselor and administrator to your classroom to tell the students about the policy and procedures for harassment issues. Send the information home to parents to read and have them sign the sheet stating they read the policies. This is common procedure in many schools to legally meet the requirement of a student's right to know.

898. Ask your administration what the beliefs are about violence in your school. Violence can and will occur anywhere if the adults in the school have not established an environment of safety.

899. Invite guest speakers to your classroom to share their experiences of racism and discrimination. Visit with the speakers prior to the presentation so both of you have a clear understanding of what you want the outcome to be for the class.

900. Learn about peer mediation. Students speak highly of their peer's involvement in conflict if it is done well. Students must be trained in mediation skills before being named peer mediators.

901. Be aware of the human rights organizations in your community and have them speak to your students. Chances are the bias exists beyond the school day and the students need to be aware of outside assistance.

902. The emotional well-being of your students can be challenging for everyone concerned. As a teacher you have support to help you with the emotions in your classroom. Enlist the help of the school nurse, counselor, and at-risk coordinator. If they do not have the skills to recommend what to do, they will know of resources that can assist.

903. Work with the school counselor to start socially appropriate behavior focus groups. The counselor should have the skills to deal with socially inappropriate behaviors and teach strategies to students to understand how to treat each other with respect and dignity.

904. Address any rumors, conversation, or notes that you encounter by making leadership aware of the context of the information. Alone the information may not appear to be important but collectively in a greater context, the content may be meaningful.

905. Noise level in a classroom can escalate to bring the worst out in anyone. Distinguish between inside and outside voices. Establish rules such as no shouting across the room, talking in a conversational voice face-to-face, and responding in class with a clear, articulate voice. School is the student's professional workplace, and the noise level of twenty or more students in a room must be monitored for the respect of everyone in the room.

906. The same noise level rules should exist in the hallways, cafeteria, and on the bus. The exceptions to the conversational voice would be cheering at school events and possibly recess and the gymnasium.

907. High noise level can also be reflected in the movement of furniture and the closing of doors and windows. Teach them to be good stewards of school property. Have the students meet the custodial staff and establish a partnership of keeping the school in great shape. Do not assume students know how to pick up after themselves or enter and leave a building in a respectful manner.

908. Most schools have some type of locker or storage system where students keep their things. Often they must share, so space is minimal. Establish the habit to clean out their lockers or desks at the end of every week and take home dirty clothes, throw away old papers, and anything else that does not need to be in school.

909. Have a suggestion box in your room for students to write recommendations that would improve school. They do not have to sign their names; you will read them privately and consider reasonable recommendations.

910. Review your school handbook for student grievances about grades. Establish with your class the process if a student should not agree with the grade they have received. If you should become involved in a grade dispute, document your meetings, the date, and issues of concern.

911. Take a CPR or first aid class with your students or colleagues. You never know when you might need to use the information from the classes in your professional or personal life.

912. If you have a student on crutches, assign a different buddy every day to help him or her with books and lunch trays. The buddy will eat with the student and be his or her assistant for the day. Expect crutches during sports season.

913. Before leaving your room after school, check to see that windows are latched, desk and filing cabinets are secured, lights are turned off and the door is locked. When you leave the building lock the outside door and make sure that the door latches tight. Always keep safety issues in mind.

Warning!

914. If you suspect illegal behavior on the part of a student or staff member, report what you know to the school counselor or to the administration immediately. Keeping this information to yourself may only exacerbate the possible problem. Behaviors to watch for are abuse, pornography, and drug use. If you suspect abuse of any kind or drug use, report your suspicions.

915. If you suspect a student to be suicidal, contact a counselor and/or the administration immediately. A life is endangered and you have a moral responsibility to report what you know.

916. You may learn about a suicidal student through one of his or her friends. Encourage the friend to go with you to the counselor or school nurse and discuss the best way to approach the situation. The suicidal student may not want to involve authority, but the symptoms cannot be ignored and need to be addressed immediately.

917. Do not drive students anywhere alone. Have someone else in the car with you at all times. Try to avoid driving students, unless you are the bus driver, have a bus driver license, school vehicle, or others with you.

918. Do not enter or check a restroom/locker room of the opposite sex. Always have someone of the same sex check the restroom and locker room areas. Do not leave yourself vulnerable to any potentially questionable situations.

919. Bullying is not new and neither are the effects it has on students. What is new is the attention it is receiving in our schools to stop it and the research-based recommendations to bully-proof your schools.

920. Be aware that bullying contributes to low self-esteem, depression, lower attendance rates, and higher rates of crime.

921. Bullying can look different at various levels of school. In the primary grades it may start with stealing someone's hat at recess or name-calling. As the years progress it can include social exclusion, threats, stalking, stealing, or physical and/or emotional harm.

922. As a teacher, invite your administration and school counselor to visit with your class at the beginning of the school year concerning the harassment policy and procedures of the school district. Post the written information in your room. You do not want your students to say they were unaware of the school policies.

923. Once you have reviewed the school's bullying and harassment policies with your class as a whole, meet with your students in small groups to discuss how to bully-proof your classroom. Student ownership is the most effective means to curtail bullying in your classroom. Provided the opportunity, they will come up with great suggestions stemming from their personal experiences.

924. Post student's quotes or slogans in the classroom as reminders that they want a safe, caring, bully-free environment in which to learn.

925. Let parents or guardians know if their child is bullying others. If you have any concern that the conversation will not go well, do not hesitate to have the school counselor and administration attend the meeting to support you. Document the date and a summary of the conversation.

926. Take seriously any verbal or written threats that threaten the safety of you or other students. Let the school counselor and administration know about the threats. The administrator should also contact law enforcement in your community. They may have had reports before concerning the same student and your information could be another piece to the puzzle of frightening behaviors.

927. Use role-playing to create under-standing of what bullying feels like for both the bystander and the person being bullied. It can also serve as an example of what behaviors are considered bullying.

928. A schoolwide program with parental and community involvement is the most effective way to bully-proof your school. If that is not happening, educate yourself on current bullying research and if you have older students, have them do the same and report back to the class.

929. Bully-proof your classroom and make your students be active bystanders if bullying occurs. Your school will have zero tolerance policies in their handbooks, but it will be up to the teacher to actually enforce the policies. You are legally responsible to provide a safe environment for your students and bully-proofing your classroom is one aspect of the safe environment.

930. Observe the quality of interaction between students at break times, in the hallways, at the bus stop, and at student activi-ties. Have students role-play the difference of appro-priate and inappropriate conversation that occur outside of the classroom. It will teach them how to react to such behavior in an appropriate manner.

931. Let students know from the beginning that disrespectful words will not be tolerated in your classroom or your school. Post quotes about respect and care around your classroom and your building. In the younger grades remind students to be the PCK kids—polite, courteous, and kind.

932. Involve students in the process of bully-proofing your school. They are the best advocates of a safe environment. Involve them in the rule-making discussion and have them do the research about the consequences that have occurred in other schools as a result of bullying.

933. Do not leave your class unattended. Students report that when the teacher steps out of the classroom, bullying will likely occur. If you must leave the classroom either call the office for assistance or tell the teacher closest to you in proximity.

934. In the classroom, in the hallway, and in other areas of the school building and grounds, keep your eyes moving. A quick glance can stop a potentially harmful situation. This is an easy way to stop actions student might regret later. Be sure to report any misbehavior to the administration and talk with the student.

935. All communities are to have a written and workable crisis plan. Make yourself aware of what to do with your students if there should be crisis, causing students to leave school early. A crisis can be defined as any event that puts your students at a safety risk.

936. Ask families to share with their children what they are to do if there is a crisis while they are in school. On their parent registration form there should be emergency information with a contact and phone number.

937. The office keeps the registration forms with parental contact information, but it would be helpful for you to keep a note card with emergency contacts in your desk. It is better to have it on a card and accessible in case of an emergency.

938. As the teacher you will be responsible for all of your students if there is an early dismissal due to inclement weather. If you cannot stay until your last student leaves, inform your administration and make sure safety for your students is taken care of before you leave.

939. Ask the office if there are any plans for the younger students pertaining to early dismissals and emergency situations. Who is responsible for the students? What if a student is left at school? Whose responsibility is this? You are responsible for your students' welfare at all times and need to have all of the information available.

940. Make sure students know phone numbers for an emergency, such as when to call 911. Have someone from the crisis center in your community speak to your students about appropriate times to use emergency numbers and what happens when they use the numbers inappropriately.

Safe School Audits

941. A safe school audit is a checklist of safety issues that will provide a framework for purchases and work details that needs to be completed for your building to meet safety standards. School districts do not always have the funds to do major repairs and renovations at once, so planning ahead is essential.

942. Work with the administration and other teachers to create a safe school team. The safe school team should consist of custodial staff, administration, teachers, students, parents, and community members. Each member of the committee brings a different safety perspective to the table.

943. The committee should tour the building at the beginning and end of the year to seek out potential safety issues. They should make a list of recommendations to be given to the administration.

944. Immediate and everyday repair should be the primary focus of this team; however, emotional and well-being safety issues can also be addressed through this committee and submitted to the school board for consideration. The questions on the survey should ask things such as:

- Do you feel safe when you leave the building at night?
- Is the parking lot properly lit?
- Are you being teased on the bus?
- Are drugs being sold in your school?

945. The make up of the safe school committee is empowering in itself, and it has an opportunity to make a difference in the safety of your students and others using the facility.

946. If your school does not have a safe school team, consider starting one with the assistance of your students, especially if you are hearing complaints about safety issues. You and your students can create a survey with safety questions addressing facilities and emotional safety. The committee does the safe school walk. Utilizing walk-through data and safe school recommendations from the committee will provide enough information for a safe school plan for your school. The plan can have a one to three year timeline based on urgency and funds.

Playground Safety

947. Almost all schools have a playground. Wherever students gather to have fun, it needs to be safe. If you have playground duty, you are responsible for the safety of the students while they are under your care.

948. Be aware that the ground cover for students on a playground is a huge issue. There seems to be no perfect ground cover, and all of them can cause injury when a student falls.

949. Make sure students know the boundaries of the area where they can play. If space allows, map out an area for ballgames, equipment, sidewalk games, and a quiet area for students to visit or read.

950. If you have recess duty, do not leave your post unattended. It is a huge responsibility and the risk of an accident is high.

951. Make sure the school nurse has the recess schedules so he or she can schedule to be available in her office at that time of the day.

952. Keep a storage bin with your classroom balls, jump ropes, and bats by the door. Be sure to mark all of the items with the school's name and grade level on the item.

953. If students take items out to the playground, they are responsible for returning the items to the storage bin at the end of recess.

954. Observe for exclusion behaviors on the playground and possible cliques forming. This is a high-bully area during that time of day. Be available to listen and visit with your students. They may be more likely to open up to you about concerns they're having in a more casual setting.

955. In cold weather, make sure you are dressed appropriately. The students will stay warm because they are active. Your job is not as active and you will become cold sooner than your students if you are not dressed for the season. Wear comfortable shoes.

956. If students do not have appropriate dress for the playground, ask the school nurse for any extra mittens or hats he or she may have in his or her office.

957. Playground equipment needs to be checked for loose bolts and weaknesses every month. When you are supervising on the playground be proactive and look for equipment defects.

958. Be sure to enforce school rules about the playground equipment. These rules are likely to include things such as only going down the slide one student at a time and not walking in front of, or behind, the swings.

959. Wear a fanny pack to recess with an emergency first aid kit inside for emergencies. The school should provide the prepared fanny pack for all recess duty teachers. If your school does not provide one, create your own. This is essential to student safety.

960. Solicit trustworthy volunteers to be on the playground with you to teach and play games with the students. It is important students learn the correct rules for the games to help with the fairness issues that will arise. This also provides you, and the school, with another set of eyes during recess.

961. As faculty, and with input from parents, establish what is appropriate attire for the playground. Do the students have to wear boots when it is muddy and snowy? Decide as a staff, in conjunction with your custodial staff, what students should do with their muddy shoes and boots after recess. Do they leave them outside of their classroom door on newspapers? These are questions that need to be decided before boot-wearing weather.

962. The administration will decide what wind chill will determine if it is inside or outside recess for the day. Most school secretaries will call the local radio station and find out the wind chill. The school will have established a degree of outdoor weather tolerance. As a classroom teacher, be prepared for indoor recess activities. Start collecting a box of board games, card games, and other activities students can do indoors that will be a break from their classroom routine, but also not disruptive inside the building.

Be an Information Gatekeeper

963. Student information is private. Students' records should be kept in a fireproof file cabinet. There should be a sign-out sheet to record anyone who looks at the files.

964. Parents might ask you for a class list of student addresses for birthday invitations. As thoughtful as this sounds you can only distribute the class roster with the student names. There cannot be any other information distributed from the school.

965. If the community newspaper visits the school and takes any pictures of students they must have a signed permission slip from the parents. Ask that they email you any pictures before they publish in the paper for proper identification, and you need to ask permission from the parents for publication.

Managing Field Trips

966. Permission slips are needed for any field trips. When taking a field trip, plan for no more than two or three children to an adult. Have the list of names, name tags, and field trip etiquette on a notepad or clipboard for each chaperone. Send thank-you notes to the chaperones following the field trip.

967. If possible, have the school pack bag lunches for the students and leave them in coolers until lunchtime. It is one thing less to worry about on an educational trip.

968. Keep attire for the field trip simple. If the students have school uniforms, have them wear those. If not, have them wear sweatshirts that display the school logo. When you have thirty students at the zoo the same time of the year other schools in the area are taking field trips, it is easier to keep track of the students from your school if they are dressed somewhat similar.

969. Name tags should have the student's name, school, and phone number on the identification tag should they become separated from the group.

970. Know how many students are on your bus and in your groups. Have the adults help you count when students re-enter the bus or meet at designated places.

971. Schools practice bus drills once a semester with the transportation staff, students, and staff. Students board the bus at the front and leave out the back exit door. They need to be taught the purpose of an emergency exit door and when and why it is used. Older students usually sit in the back. A bus is just like an airplane, if the older students sit close to the exit they are responsible to help everyone exit if needed.

972. As a teacher, help the bus driver enforce the safety rules. Students and parents need to be aware of the bus rules, especially if a student has a bus-riding violation filed and it jeopardizes him or her from riding the bus to school.

973. Arrival and dismissal of the school day can be chaotic if procedures are not established. There needs to be signage for bus parking, and drop-off and pick-up points for cars so everyone is aware of the safety rules. Students need to know where they can walk and not walk when arriving and leaving the school grounds.

974. Dismissal is an exciting part of the day and can be a disaster if traffic patterns and procedures are not planned. Teachers will be expected to be involved with the arrival and dismissal of students. The presence of adults helps control the excitement.

975. Students need to know what bus they are to ride and teachers need a roster with the name of the bus driver and other students on the route.

976. Bus drivers may assign seats, at least at the beginning of the year, so they can learn their riders' names. Have your students wear nametags with their bus numbers on it until the students and driver become familiar with the routine.

977. Some students are walkers, and others will possibly be riding with high school brothers or sisters. Refer to the student's fall registration form and write on the information card you have in your file how the student will be coming and going from school.

978. If there is a change in the student's travel routine, the parent/guardian needs to let you and the school secretary know of the change with a written note or face-to-face conversation. This is for safety reasons.

979. If the high school parking lot is near your grade school, ask if the city police can patrol the area in the morning and the afternoon for speeding and reckless driving. The police's presence will slow down the departure at the end of the day.

Safety Drills

980. Every school must have at least one fire drill a year, if not two. The fire department might attend one of the fire drills and observe your procedures and the speed that your students exit the building.

981. Take any drill seriously. As a new teacher, ask what the procedures are for your classroom. There should be lit exit signs and an exit map posted by the door of your classroom for any drill your school practices. Always have a class list and schedule with you when you leave the building so you can check when you arrive at your designated spot that all of your students exited the building safely.

982. Learn what the procedures are for bomb threats and how to signal for danger if you need to.

983. In most schools only the front door is unlocked during the day, and all guests must sign in at the office. If you invite guests to the school, remind them to check in with the office before going to the classroom. The office will have visitor nametags and a roster to sign in and out.

984. There should be a few visitor parking spots and a welcome sign on the front door telling visitors where the office is and to check into the office when they arrive.

Encourage Good Behavior outside of the Classroom as Well as Within

985. Establish cafeteria rules the first day of school. Form a partnership with the food service staff so they are glad to see your class in the cafeteria. No teacher wants the class that is known for leaving a mess on the table and floor before they leave. Treat the cafeteria like a fine restaurant.

986. School activities such as athletic events are opportunities to teach good sportsmanship and social skills. Ask the athletic department what your welcoming plan is for visiting teams. Some schools actually have students that are not athletes greeting the team bus when it arrives and escorting the visiting team to the locker rooms.

987. To encourage appropriate behavior among your students offer free admission to students who volunteer to be part of a welcoming group. Tell them they are expected to wear some type of school polo shirt or jacket with the school logo. Not only is this an important job within the school, it also gives someone that wants to be involved with athletics that may not be athletic, a chance to be part of the group.

988. Schools often host music and speech competitions once or twice a year. Encourage the same behavior you would expect at an athletic event. This is also a good time to involve some of the students that are not actively participating with the fine arts to learn more about the fine arts activities. Students are very capable of hosting a performance room, timing the events, assisting the judges, and recording the ratings. It is also important to have a person greet the buses, welcome the visitors to your school, and guide them on arrival and departure locations.

989. You want to be the school that other schools want to come to for activities. You want your events to be well organized and the school staff and students to be friendly. You want to set an example of good behavior and sportsmanship.

990. Students that feel included and that they are part of the system are much more likely to do better academically. As a teacher, be aware of all school events, and encourage student participation from all students.

991. If you are a coach, be aware of the rules of the sport you are coaching so your students will have the same equal opportunity as everyone else in the league. Stress the importance of these rules and sportsmanship behavior on the playing field.

992. Work with your athletic department, and make sure your equipment and uniforms are in the best shape possible. Check for any safety rules for equipment like your football helmets or other protective gear.

993. If you are the swim coach, work with the custodial staff concerning chemical levels in the pool water. Also, be sure to have an appropriate student to adult ratio when in the pool area. Find out what certifications you need and work with your administration to ensure that appropriate safety measures are taken in the pool area.

Dealing with Death in the School

994. The death of a student is the ultimate tragedy you will deal with as a teacher. The day you learn of the death of a student will stay with you forever. You are the adult and you will have to lead the grieving process for your students.

995. Work with your administration to ensure that there are grief counselors and trained professionals to help you and your students. Involve the parents because they may need help dealing with the loss and with their child at home.

996. When you learn of the tragedy, meet with your class and ask for suggestions of support for the grieving family. This may include taking food to the house, sharing pictures with the family, writing stories or cards to help them remember what they loved most about their classmate or friend, and giving to the family. If possible, attend the funeral or the wake with your students and their families.

997. It is good to get back to a routine as soon as possible, but by no means will this student be forgotten. Honor the student's life with a remembrance in the school paper or yearbook. If there is a memorial donation, visit with the family and honor their wishes. Their wishes might include a scholarship or a tree or bench on the school grounds.

998. Memorials are a nice celebration to plan on the student's birthday or anniversary of their death. Work with your school administration, counselor, and the student's family on appropriate timing for such a generous and thoughtful donation to the school in the student's memory.

999. The death of a student's family member is also very traumatic. Meet with the class and discuss how you can be supportive of the classmate in his or her time of sadness. Students will often not know what to say. Explain to them that it is important to be present and that just saying "I'm sorry" is often enough.

1000. It is important to be present with your students, their families, and your friends when going through any kind of grief or loss. Young people need to know that people take care of each other in a crisis. It is okay to cry, hug, and laugh. All ages have the ability to feel a sense of loss.

Appendix

National Middle School Association (NMSA)

Association for Supervision and
Curriculum Development

National Education Association

Association for Childhood Education

Council for Exceptional Children

International Reading Association

National Science Teachers Association

National Council of Teachers of English

Association of Science-Technology Centers

National Council for the Social Studies

Online Lesson Plans

http://www.mcrel.org/resources/links/hotlinks.asp

http://www.school.discovery.com

http://ldonline.org

http://lessonplanz.com

http://ericir.syr.edu/Virtual/Lessons

http://www.bigchalk.com

http://www.education-world.com/a_lesson/

http://coollesson.org/

http://theideabox.com/

http://teacher.scholastic.com/resources/

http://teachersnetwork.org/

http://pacificnet.net/

http://www.abcteach.com/

http://www.lessonplans.com/

http://TeacherPlanet.com/

http://KidZone.ws

http://www.theteacherscorner.net

Free Items
http://justfreestuff.com/teacher.html

http://thefrugalshopper.com/

http://freakyfreddies.com/teacher.htm

http://timesaversforteachers.com/

Learning Support
www.tolerance.org/hidden-bias/index.html

Preventing Classroom Bullying:
http://www.interventioncentral.org

Olweus Bullying Prevention Program:
http://virtual.clemson.edu/groups/ncri.pdfs/bullying
fact sheet2.pdf

http://bullystoppers.com/101-great-comeback-
lines.htm

Center for the Study and Prevention of Violence:
http://www.colorado.edu/cspv/factsheets

Educational Equity Concepts, Inc.: http://www.edequity.org/resum.htm

United Learning: 1-800-323-9084, www.unitedlearning.com

Peacebuilders (Grades k-8): 877-473-2236, www.peacebuilders.com

Johnson Institute, Hazelden: 1-800-328-9000, www.hazelden.org

A module of Teenage Health Teaching Modules (THTM) Education Development Center, Inc.: 800-225-4276 ext. 2737, www.edc.org

National Institute of Mental Health: http://http://www.nimh.nih.gov/

U.S. Department of Education http://www.ed.gov/

http://www.eslkidstuff.com/

Books to Read

Barth, R.S.,(1990). *Improving Schools from Within.* New York: Jossey Bass Publisher.

Bender, Y., (2003). *The New Teacher's Handbook.* Norwich, VT: Nomad Press.

Burke, K. (2001). *Tips for Managing Your Classroom.* Arlington Heights, IL: Skylight Professional Development.

Carson, R., (2003). *The Don't Sweat Guide for Teachers.* New York, NY: Hyperion.

Chapman, C. & King, R. (2003). *Differentiated Instructional Strategies for Reading in the Content Areas.* Thousand Oaks, CA: Corwin Press, Inc.

Charles, C.M., (2002). *Essential Elements of Effective Discipline.* Boston, MA: Allyn & Bacon.

Coloroso, B. (2002). *Kids Are Worth It! Giving Your Child the Gift of Inner Discipline.* Harper Collins Publishing.

Daniels, H. & Bizar, M. (2005). *Teaching the Best Practice Way.* Portland, ME: Stenhouse Publishers.

Esquith, R. (2003). *There Are No Shortcuts.* New York: Pantheon Books.

Finkel, D. Y., (2000). *Teaching with Your Mouth Shut.* Portsmouth, NH: Boynton/Cook Publishers.

Ginsberg, M. B. & Wlodkowski, R.J. (2000). *Creating Highly Motivating Classrooms for All Students.* San Francisco, CA: Jossy-Bass.

Gregory, G.H. (2003). *Differentiated Instructional Strategies in Practice.* Thousand Oaks, CA: Corwin Publishing, Inc.

Heacox, D. (2002). *Differentiating Instruction in the Regular Classroom.* Minneapolis, MN: Free Spirit Press, Inc.

Jensen, E. (1998). *Teaching with the Brain in Mind.* Alexandria, VA: Association Of Supervision and Curriculum Development.

Kohn, A., (1999). *The Schools Our Children Deserve.* New York: Houghton Mifflin, Co.

Marzano, R.J., Marzano, J.S., & Pickering, D.J. (2003). *Classroom Management That Works.* Alexandria, VA: Association of Supervision and Curriculum Development.

Marzano, R.J., Pickering D. J. & Pollock J.E. (2001). *Classroom Instruction That Works.* Alexandria, VA: Association of Supervision and Curriculum Development.

Naegle, P. (2002). *The New Teacher's Complete Sourcebook Middle School.* New York,NY: Scholastic Professional Books.

Partin, R. L. (2005). *Classroom Teacher's Survival Guide.* San Francisco, CA: Jossey-Bass.

Roehrig, A.D., Pressleu, M. & Talotta, D.A. (2002). *Stories of Beginning Teachers.* Notre Dame, IN: University of Notre Dame Press.

Rominger, L., Packard, S.L. & Elkin, N. (2001). *Your First Year As a High School Teacher.* Roseville, CA: Prima Publishing.

Sadler, C.R. (2001). *Comprehension Strategies for Middle Grade Learners.* Newark, DE: International Reading Association.

Sarasin L.C., (1999). *Learning Style Perspectives Impact in the Classroom.* Madison, WI: Atwood Publishing.

Shalaway, L. (1998). *Learning to Teach...Not Just for Beginners.* Jefferson City, MO: Scholastic.

Sousa, D.A. (1995). *How the Brain Learns.* Reston, VI: The National Association of Secondary School Principal.

Thorson S.A. (2003). *Listening to Students: Reflections on Secondary Classroom Management.* Boston, MA: Allyn & Bacon.

Wiggins, G. & McTighe, J. 1998. Alexandria, VA: Association for Supervision and Curriculum Development.

Willever L. F. & Lisa Battinelli. (2002). *On Your Mark, Get Set, Teach!* Trenton, N.J.: Franklin Mason Press.

Wong, H.K. & Wong, R. T. (1998). *The First Days of School.* Mountain View, CA: Harry K. Wong Publications, Inc.

Wood, C., and Peter Wrenn (1999). *Time to Teach Time to Learn. Changing the Pace of School.* Northeast Foundation on Children, Inc.

Yanoff, J.C. (2001). *The Excellent Teacher's Handbook.* Chicago, IL: Arthur Coyle Press.

Index

A

administrator, 2, 3, 4
    initiative, 239
assessment, learning, 123, 124, 126–128
    standardized tests, 128–133
    student involvement, 136–138
attendance, 5, 30, 50, 51, 165
    absent students, 9
    tardy students, 51, 52

B

behavior problems, 40, 56, 62, 65
    behavior contracts, 59
    behavior management, 55
    bullying, 56, 283–286, 292
    conflicts, 56
    consequences, 54, 58, 62, 64, 70
    detention, 65
    discipline, 5, 57
    fights, 64
    harassment, 56, 276
    involving parents, 58, 66, 67
    nonverbal cues, 60, 61
    outside resources, 67, 68
    preventing, 57
    solutions, 66, 278, 284
building layout, 2, 4, 5

C

D

E

ESL students, 163, 164, 167

    classroom, 177–179

    communication, 174–177

    educate yourself, 181–185

    language partners, 180, 181

    teaching, 169–174

    terms, 166

        Basic Interpersonal Communication Skills, 167

        Cognitive Academic Language Proficiency, 167

        English language learners, 165, 166, 168, 172, 176

        Language Proficiency Level, 167

        Limited English Proficient student (LEP), 166

        Non-English Proficient student (NEP), 166

extracurricular activities, 54

F

field trips, 19, 240, 241, 295, 296

forms, 6, 30

G

grading, 113–115

    documenting, 138, 139, 140

H

M

materials, 8
mentoring program, 6
mission statement, 3
    goals, 4

N

note taking, 86
nurse, 11, 12, 282, 291
    first aid kit, 12

O

organization, 7
    areas, 8, 9, 10
    classroom, 7, 10, 44, 47
    planner, 14, 88

P

parents, reaching out to, 209–212
    communicating, 219, 220, 224, 225
permission slips, 19
policies, 3
principal, 4, 5, 12, 13, 15, 59, 64, 216
procedures, 2, 3, 20, 50
professionalism, 231, 232, 248
    bias, 233, 236, 249
    clothing, 245, 247
    education, 238, 241, 242

About the Authors

©David's Gallery

Kathleen Brenny has a BA in education and a masters and specialist degree in administration. She owned and operated the Children's Learning Center, and was a principal at Kuemper Catholic School in Carroll, Iowa. Ms. Brenny has served on numerous educational committees at a local, state, and federal level, as well as presented at state and national conferences concerning safe school issues, assessment, early childhood, and English Language Learners. She is presently a school improvement consultant and lives in Sac City, Iowa.

©David's Gallery

Kandace Martin has been a secondary English teacher, middle school administrator, university instructor, and a staff development consultant. Throughout her thirty years in education she has supervised student teachers, taught elementary and secondary education majors, and developed and facilitated an induction and mentoring program for teachers in over fifty school districts. She has also written and presented papers at several national and state conferences. Mrs. Martin lives in Webster City, Iowa.